CW01301099

This book belongs to:

....

Text by Dr Bipasha Choudhury, Andrea Mills
Subject consultants Sammy Kornhauser, Dominique Lowenthal, Dr Kristina Routh

Project Editor Robin Moul
Editor Laura Gilbert
Senior Art Editor Charlotte Bull
Designed by Nidhi Mehra, Hannah Moore, Samantha Ricciardi, Sadie Thomas, Nehal Verma
Additional illustrations Kitty Glavin
Managing Editor Penny Smith
Deputy Art Director Mabel Chan
Publishing Director Sarah Larter
Production Editor Dragana Puvacic
Production Controller Leanne Burke
Jacket Designer Charlotte Bull
Jacket Coordinator Magda Pszuk

First published in Great Britain in 2023 by
Dorling Kindersley Limited
DK, One Embassy Gardens, 8 Viaduct Gardens,
London, SW11 7BW

The authorised representative in the EEA is
Dorling Kindersley Verlag GmbH. Arnulfstr. 124,
80636 Munich, Germany

Copyright © 2023 Dorling Kindersley Limited
A Penguin Random House Company
10 9 8 7 6 5 4 3 2
004-332925-Aug/2023

All rights reserved.
No part of this publication may be reproduced, stored in or introduced into a retrieval system, or transmitted, in any form, or by any means (electronic, mechanical, photocopying, recording, or otherwise), without the prior written permission of the copyright owner.

A CIP catalogue record for this book
is available from the British Library.
ISBN: 978-0-2415-8495-8

Printed and bound in China

For the curious
www.dk.com

MIX
Paper | Supporting responsible forestry
FSC™ C018179

This book was made with Forest Stewardship Council ™ certified paper - one small step in DK's commitment to a sustainable future. For more information go to www.dk.com/our-green-pledge

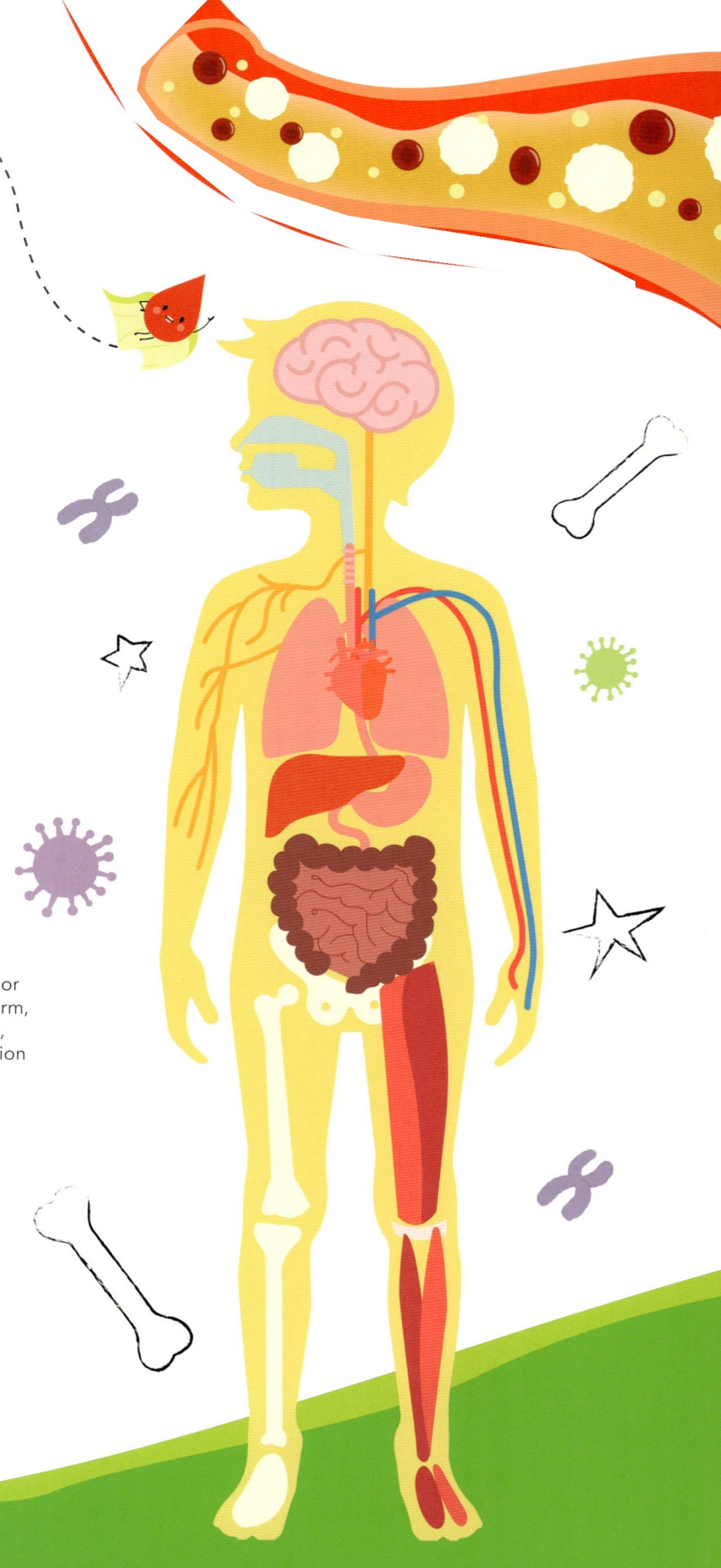

My Very IMPORTANT HUMAN BODY Encyclopedia

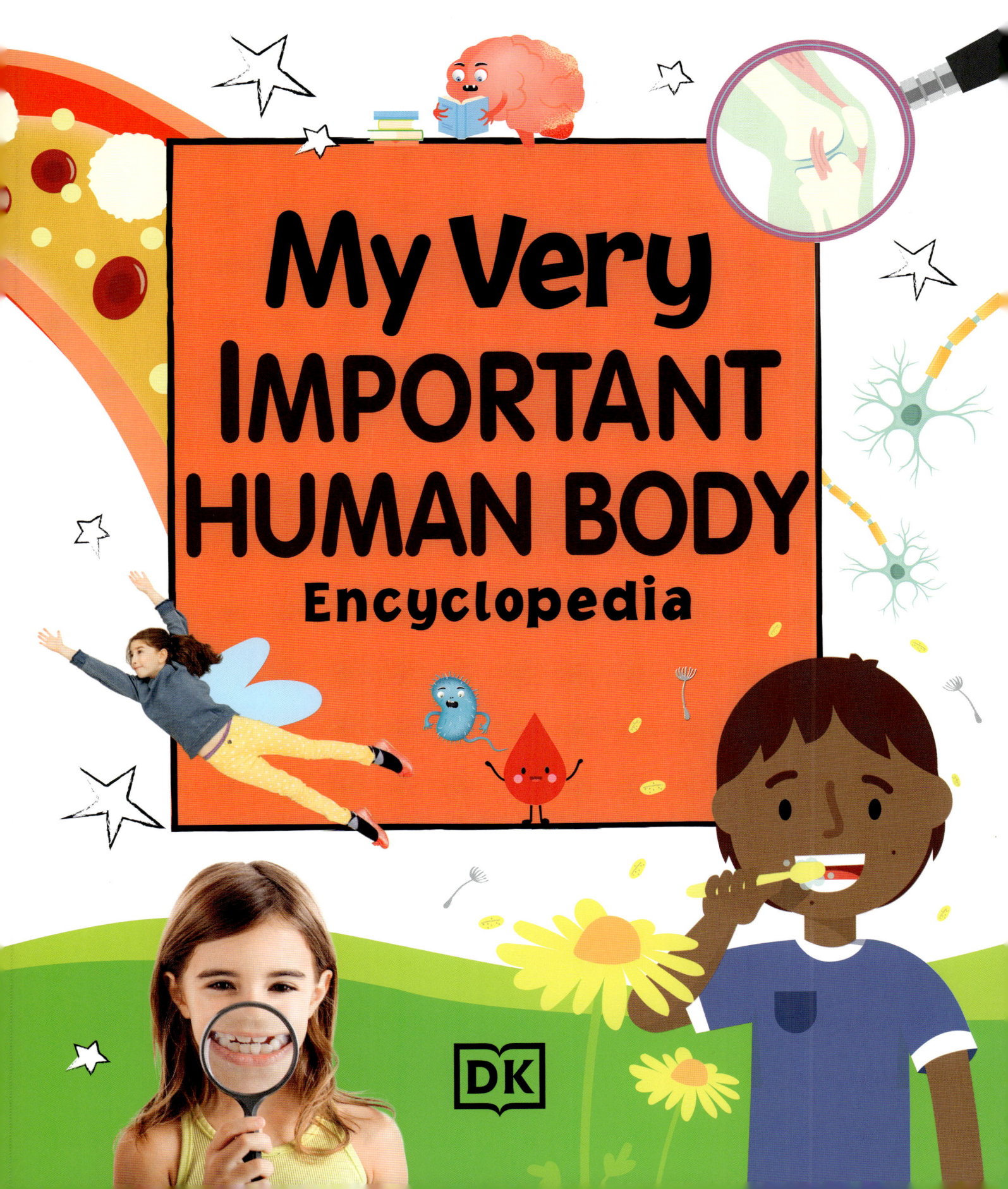

DK

Contents

Great journeys

10 Grand tour
12 Looking inside
14 Lots of layers
16 All systems go!
18 What am I made of?
20 Building blocks
22 In the genes
24 Discovering DNA
26 We can all play
28 Growing up
30 Helpful hormones
32 How long can I live?
34 Uniquely human
36 Ultimate survivors
38 Get your facts right

The body's framework

42 Extraordinary X-rays
44 Super skeleton
46 How tall can I grow?
48 Strong skull
50 Brilliant bones
52 Tough tissues
54 On the move
56 How high can I jump?
58 Nerves of steel
60 Reflex actions

62 The limbs
64 Joining in
66 Protective pelvis
68 Coming in handy
70 Hard as nails
72 Making your mark
74 Feet first

The making of me

78 Baby's beginning
80 Twins
82 Skin deep
84 Body temperature
86 Hairy story

88 Brain box
90 Lost in thought
92 Communication
94 Face to face
96 Pearly whites
98 Lots of liquids
100 Oxygen's journey
102 Take a breath
104 Heart of the matter
106 A rush of blood
108 Circulation cycle
110 Looking at lymph
112 Cleaning up
114 Eating adventure
116 Little and large
118 Drink up

Coming to your senses

- 122 **Making sense**
- 124 **Eyes**
- 126 **Vision**
- 128 **Optical illusions**
- 130 **Ears**
- 132 **Ear-splitting sounds**
- 134 **Keeping your balance**
- 136 **Nose**
- 138 **On the scent**
- 140 **Touch**
- 142 **Tip of the tongue**
- 144 **Taste**
- 146 **Yummy or yucky?**
- 148 **More marvellous senses**

What's going on?

- 152 **Early experts**
- 154 **Head lice**
- 156 **Temperature rising**
- 158 **Busy bedtime**
- 160 **Fight, flight, or freeze?**
- 162 **Coughs and sneezes**
- 164 **Germs on the go**
- 166 **Victorious vaccines**
- 168 **All about allergies**
- 170 **Hay fever season**
- 172 **Down the wrong way**
- 174 **Tummy pains**
- 176 **Sun safety**
- 178 **Sore stings**

180 **Black and blue**

182 **Cuts and scrapes**

184 **Broken bones**

186 **Lifesaving discoveries**

Living well

190 **Food for thought**

192 **Getting to know your food**

194 **Excellent exercise**

196 **Time for bed, sleepyhead**

198 **Mental health**

200 **Body talk**

202 **Body bugs**

204 **Defensive measures**

206 **Staying safe**

208 **All kitted out**

210 **Finding the fakes**

212 **At the dentist**

214 **Check-up**

216 **Space doctor**

218 **Human body words**

220 **Index**

223 **Acknowledgements**

Great journeys

Remember: diagrams of the human body get flipped, as if you are looking at another person. Their left is on your right.

What you see on your left is the right side of this person's body.

What you see on your right is the left side of this person's body.

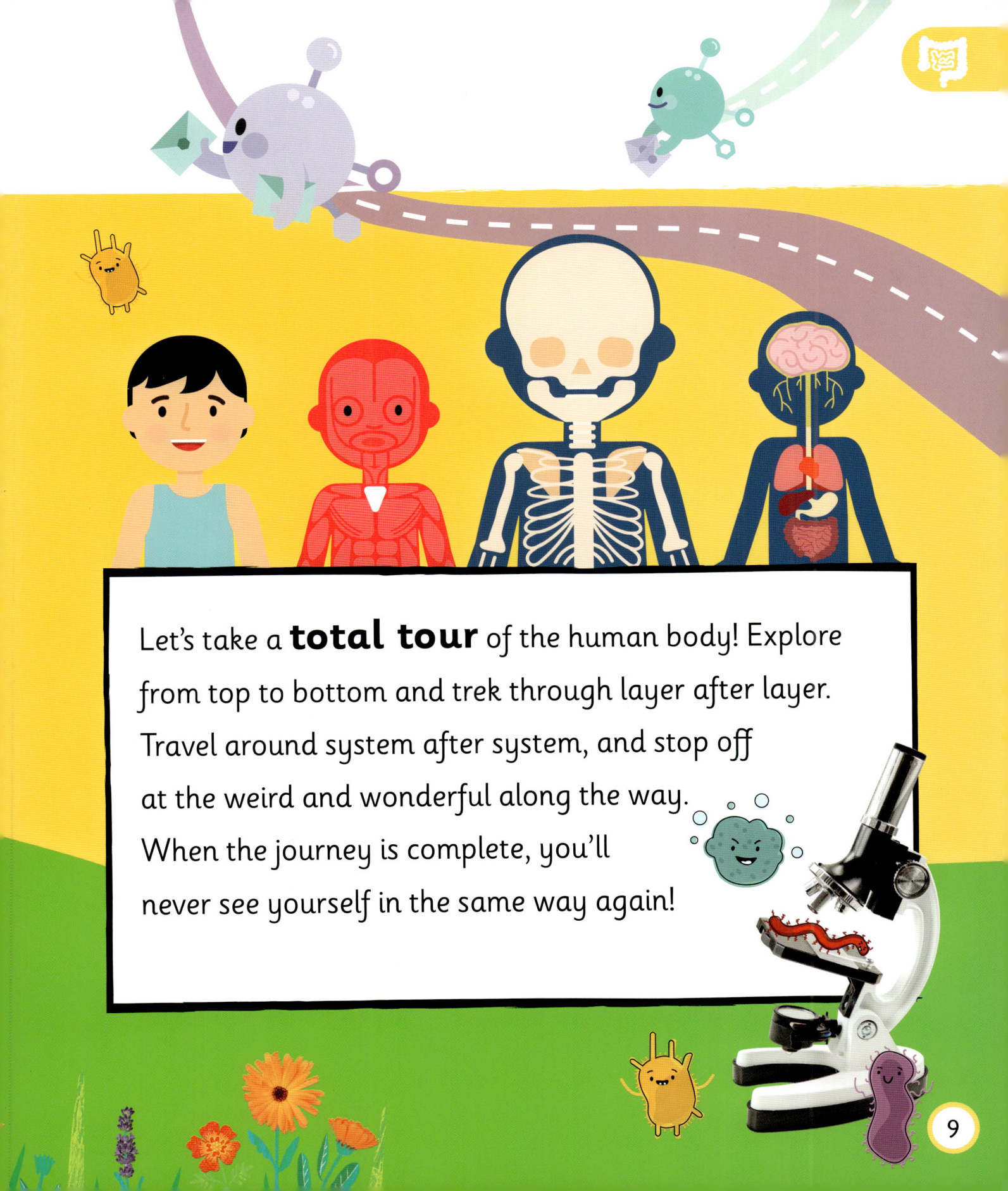

Let's take a **total tour** of the human body! Explore from top to bottom and trek through layer after layer. Travel around system after system, and stop off at the weird and wonderful along the way. When the journey is complete, you'll never see yourself in the same way again!

9

Grand tour

Get ready for your complete tour of the **human body**. You'll **explore** it in depth and in detail, from top to toe, inside and out.

Body talk
Your body is an incredible **machine** working to keep you healthy **24/7**, but how well do you know its parts and how it works? **Let's go exploring**…

On the outside
We know what the **outsides** of our bodies are like. It's harder to know about the **insides** of our bodies or minds as so much is going on.

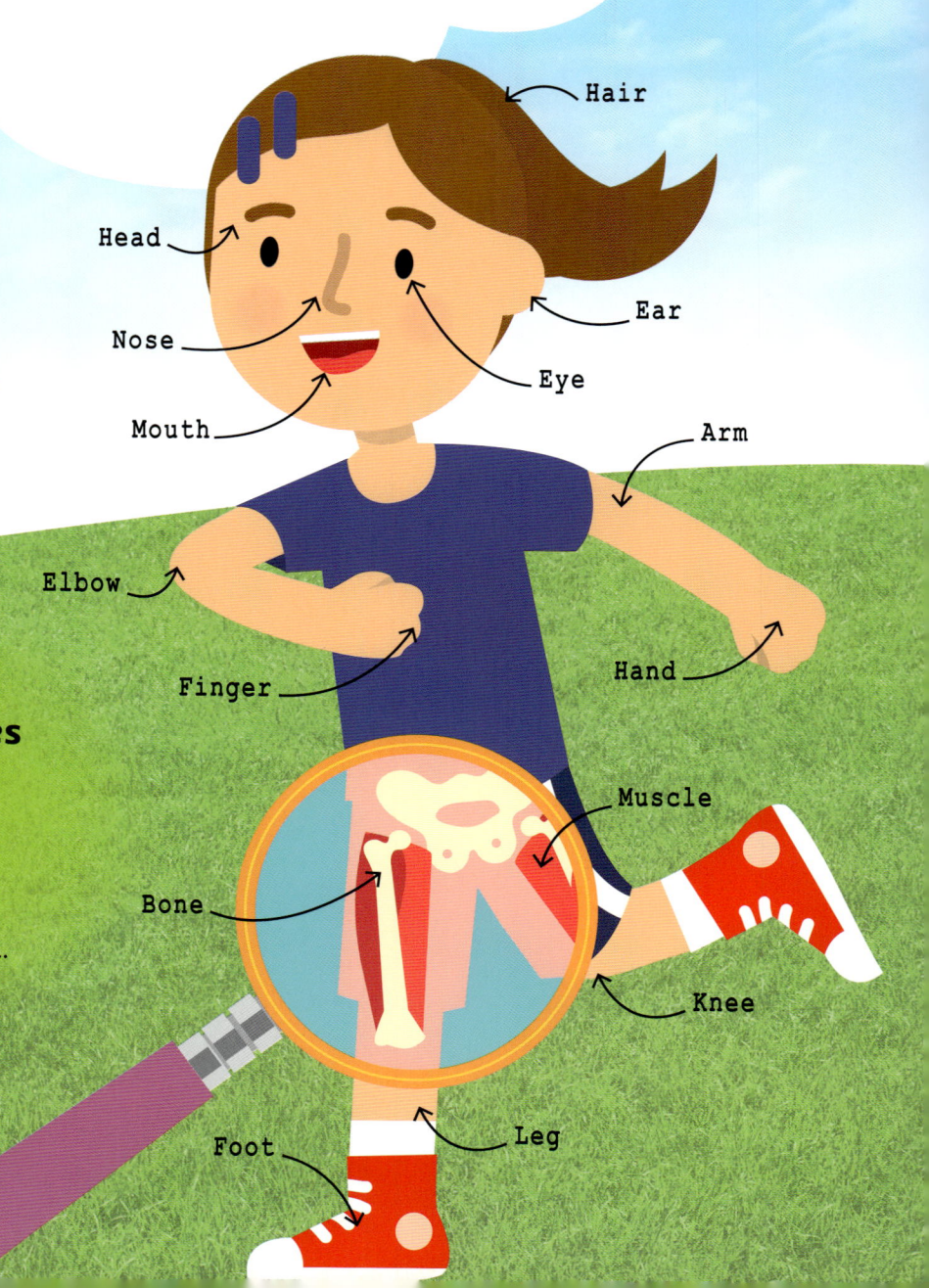

- Hair
- Head
- Nose
- Mouth
- Ear
- Eye
- Arm
- Elbow
- Finger
- Hand
- Muscle
- Bone
- Knee
- Foot
- Leg

All together

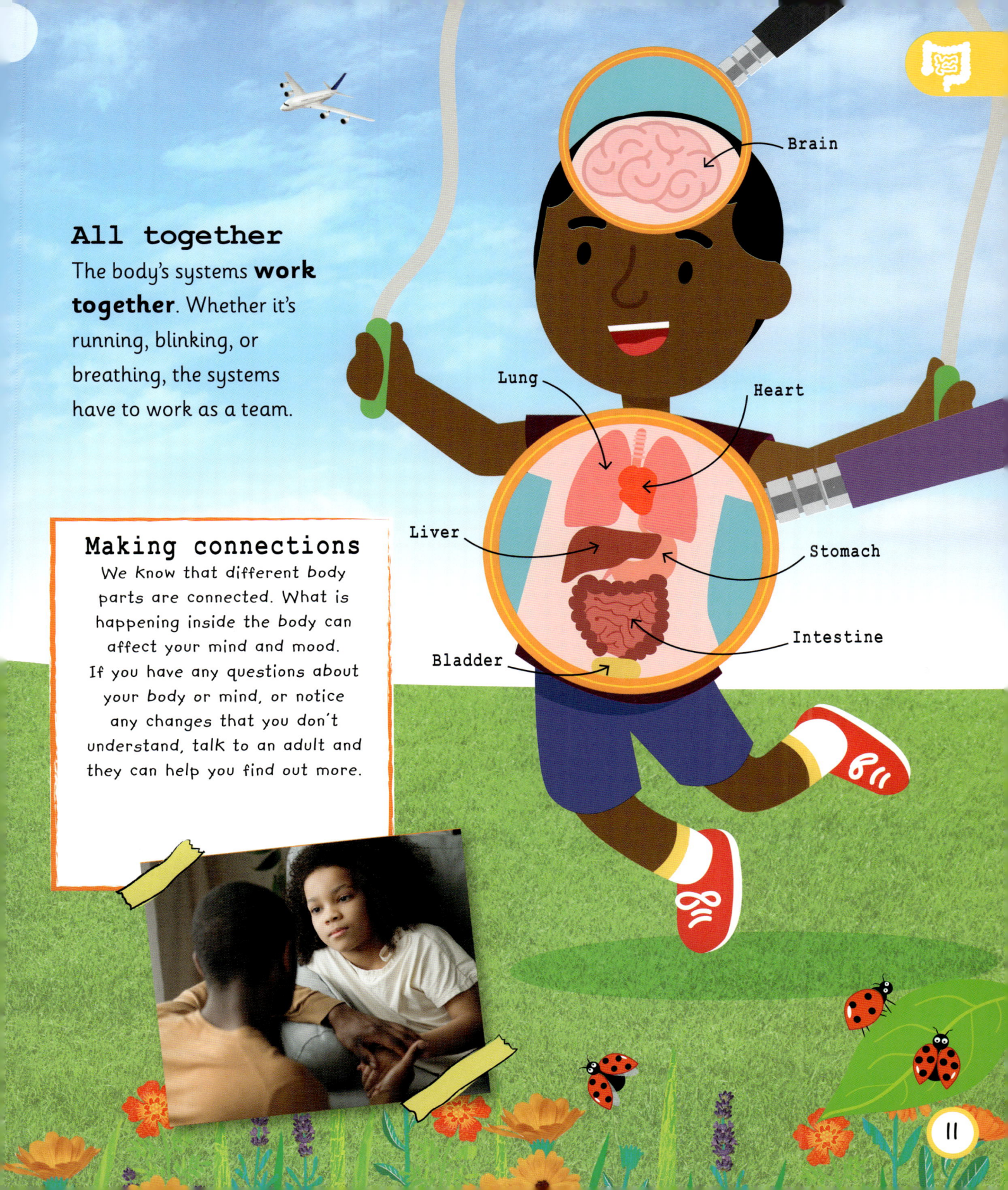

The body's systems **work together**. Whether it's running, blinking, or breathing, the systems have to work as a team.

Making connections

We know that different body parts are connected. What is happening inside the body can affect your mind and mood. If you have any questions about your body or mind, or notice any changes that you don't understand, talk to an adult and they can help you find out more.

Brain

Lung

Heart

Liver

Stomach

Bladder

Intestine

Looking inside

Amazing developments in **medical technology** make it possible to view **inside** the human body in different ways. These methods help us learn about what's going on inside us.

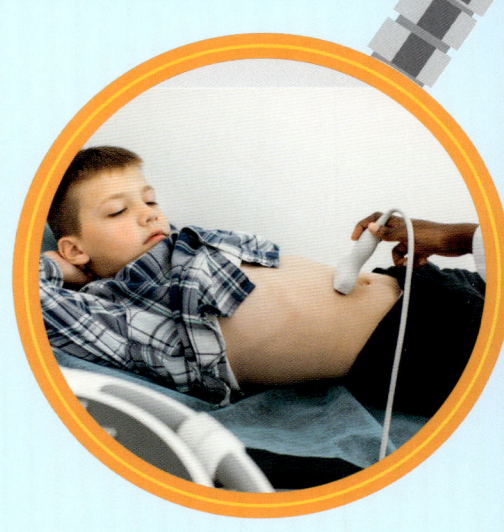

If you have tummy pain, you might have an ultrasound.

Microscope
This tool **magnifies** tiny samples from the body so they look a lot bigger. This can reveal **germs** or **diseases** in detail.

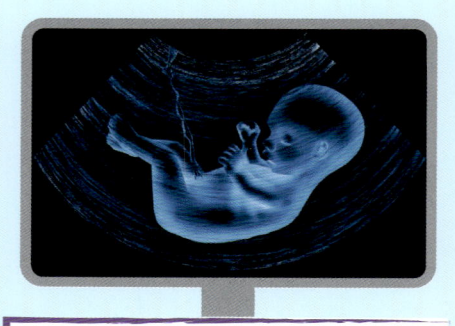

Ultrasound
This type of scan makes **pictures** of the body using sound waves. Ultrasounds are often used to **examine** babies before they are born.

EEG
Electroencephalography (EEG) studies electrical activity inside the **brain** to **diagnose** different medical conditions.

More than 3.5 BILLION X-rays are taken each year.

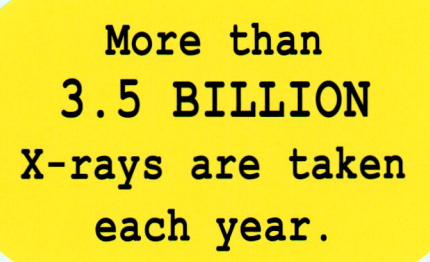

MRI
Magnetic resonance imaging (MRI) uses **magnets** and **radio waves** to scan the body, especially the brain. It can detect if the brain has been damaged.

X-ray
An X-ray machine takes pictures of hard parts of the body. This helps doctors see **breaks** in bones, and helps dentists find **decay** in teeth.

Angiogram
For this type of scan, a **medical dye** is injected into a **blood vessel**. Blood vessels usually can't be seen on an X-ray, so the dye makes them visible. Doctors can then see if there are any problems in the vessels.

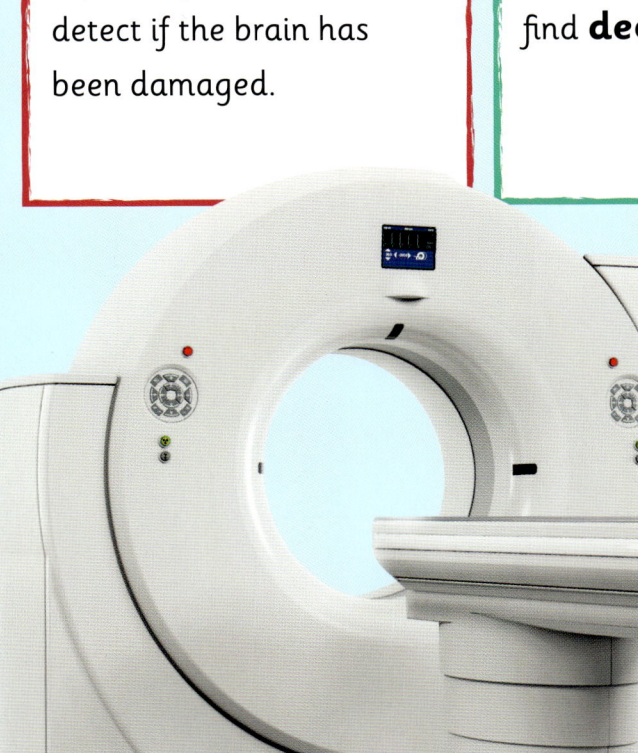

An MRI is noisy, so patients can listen to their favourite music on headphones while they get a scan.

13

Lots of layers

The skin is the only layer of the human body that is **visible**. But beneath it, there are **lots more layers**!

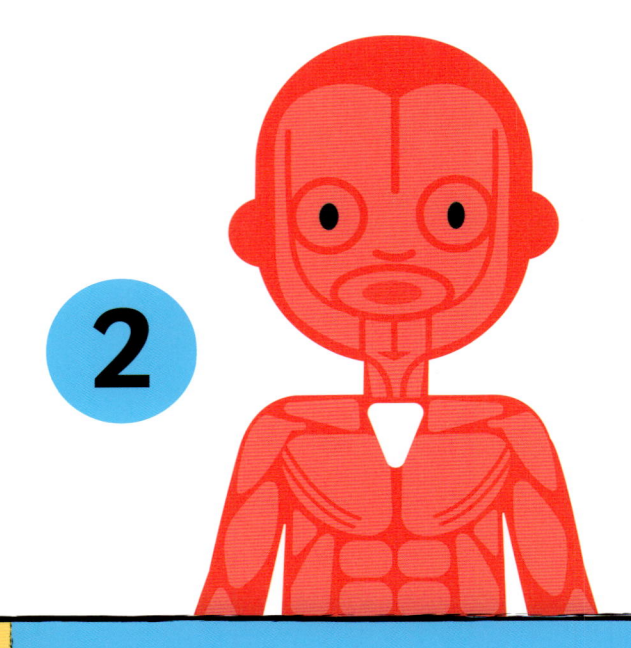

1

2

Skin is the LARGEST organ in the human body.

"MUSCLE" is named after the Latin word for "mouse".

Skin

This vast layer protects us against the outside world and provides a complete covering from head to toe. It does many jobs, including acting as a barrier so germs can't get through and helping to keep your body temperature steady.

Muscles

Under the skin are many muscles. They enable the body to move in different ways, including walking, stretching and laughing. Muscles also help other body parts do their jobs, like moving blood around the body.

Control centre

Behind the scenes, the brain is running everything. The brain processes information from other parts of the body and takes control of each thing that is going on. If there is a part of the body that isn't working, there may be an issue with the brain. Brain health is really important. This is why you must wear a helmet when riding a bike or scooter.

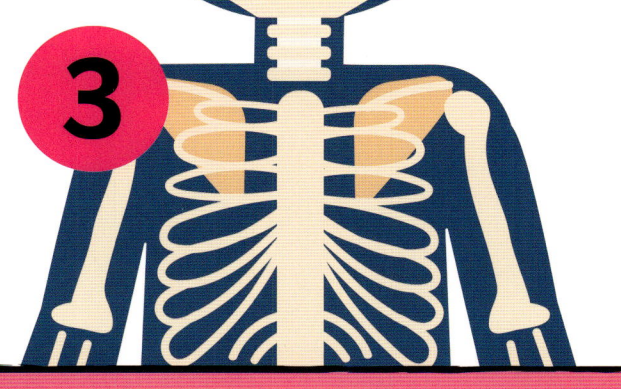

3

4

Bones and muscles make up about half the BODY'S WEIGHT.

Scientists disagree about HOW MANY organs there are!

Bones

The only thing that stops the body collapsing in a wobbly heap is the skeleton. Under the skin and muscles, hard bones create a structure for the body, so it keeps its shape, but can still move.

Organs

The body is full of parts, called organs, that each do a special task. They include the brain, lungs, liver, stomach, and intestines. The organs keep a person alive.

15

All systems go!

Your body is running **many different systems**. Each one has its own **job** to do, but also works alongside the other systems.

Super systems

Organs are **body parts** with a special function. The **brain**, **heart**, and **lungs** are all **organs**. When different organs work together in the body, they **form a system**. There are **12** systems in total.

Integumentary

This long word means the skin, hair, and nails, which come together to create the outside of the body. This system protects all the body systems inside.

Skeletal

The 206 bones of the body make up the skeletal system. Together they give the body shape, allow movement, and protect internal organs.

Nervous

One brain and billions of nerve cells make up the nervous system. This system processes information from our senses and controls our movements and reactions.

Muscular

The muscular system makes the body move. There are different types of muscles, but most are flexible muscles attached to the bones.

Lymphatic

This system cleans up a liquid called lymph to keep fluid levels balanced. It also carries blood cells that beat infections.

Digestive

The digestive system goes from the mouth to the bottom. Organs remove liquid and process food for energy, and get rid of waste as poo.

Endocrine

Hormones are chemical messengers produced by the endocrine system that help parts of the body know what to do. There are about 50 hormones that control things like growth and sleep.

Reproductive

Reproductive organs are different in both males and females, but parts from both are needed to make a baby. Babies grow inside female reproductive systems.

Female

Male

Respiratory

The lungs and surrounding airways form the respiratory system. They keep the body alive by breathing air in and out.

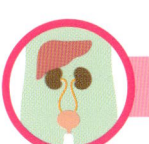

Urinary

The urinary system uses the kidneys to make urine (wee), which is stored in the bladder. When this gets full, it's time to go to the loo!

Immune

This system uses a network of organs to protect the body against harmful germs, and fight against illness and infection.

Circulatory

The heart, blood, and blood vessels make up the circulatory system. This network pumps oxygen around the body in the bloodstream and carries away waste, such as carbon dioxide.

17

What am I made of?

The body contains a huge mix of substances. There are lots of different ingredients, including plenty of **water** and even a small amount of **gold**.

More than half your body is water.

Water levels
Newborns are 75 per cent water, but this falls to about 60 per cent by **adulthood**. This is due to the fact that muscle contains more water than fat, and **older people have less muscle**.

Rise and fall
Food and drink contains water, so **water levels rise** when you eat and drink. Sweating, weeing, and breathing out loses water, so water levels fall.

You can survive for about 3 WEEKS without food,

Main ingredients

As well as **water**, the body is made up of **lots of other things**. Here are some of them:

65 per cent is oxygen
Oxygen is found in water. Having a lot of water in the body means there's also lots of oxygen.

18 per cent is carbon
The lead in pencils is made of carbon. There is enough carbon inside you to make 10,000 pencils!

10 per cent is hydrogen
Hydrogen appears in lots of chemicals inside the body, including water. This is the most common element in the universe.

3 per cent is nitrogen

Nitrogen is also an important ingredient in certain explosives!

Going for gold

Your body contains gold! You'll never find it because it **weighs less than a grain of sand** and floats in your blood. It would take the amount of gold in 40,000 people to make one gold ring!

but the body can only last 3 DAYS without water.

Building blocks

The human body is made of **teeny-tiny cells** that are too small to see. Just like with building blocks, lots of little pieces combine to make all kinds of bigger structures.

Tissues
Cells with the same job connect in **larger groups** to form tissue. This is now big enough to be seen by the human eye. **Bone**, **muscles**, and **blood** are all types of body tissues.

Tiny cells
The **smallest structure** in the human body is a cell, which can only be seen under a microscope. There are **more than 200** types of cell, such as bone cells. As you grow and get bigger, your cells **renew** and more cells are made.

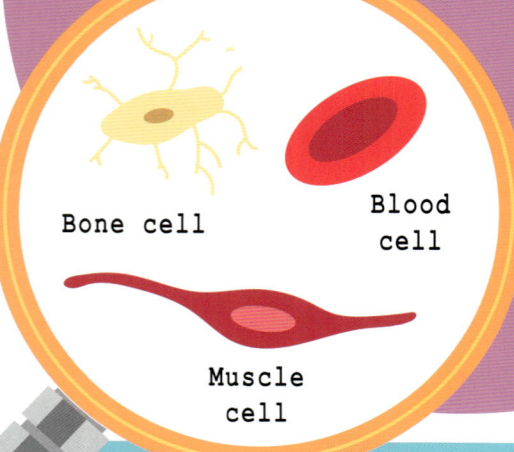

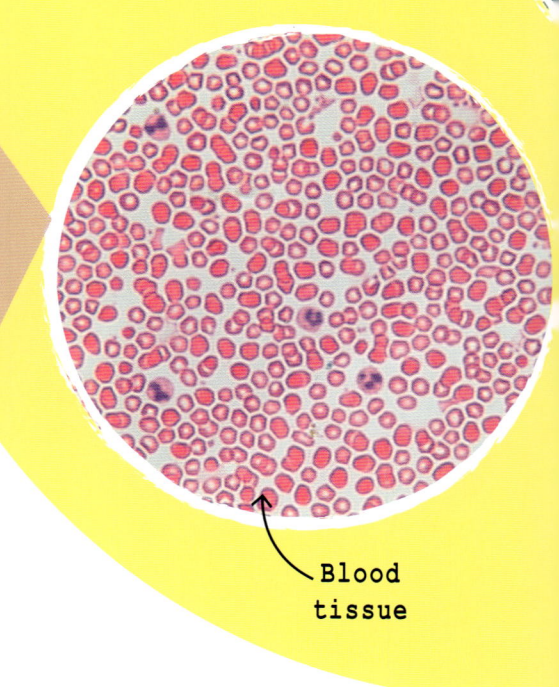

Bone cell
Blood cell
Muscle cell

Blood tissue

The average adult human has

Vital organs

Two or more tissues make **even bigger structures** in the body, called organs. These organs, such as the **brain**, **heart**, and **lungs**, are key parts of the 12 body systems. They are vital to staying alive.

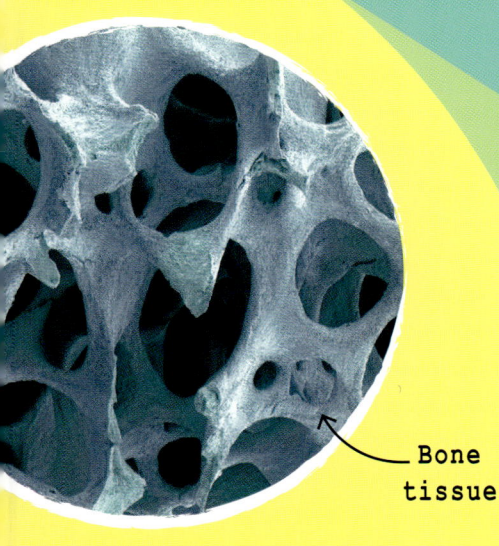

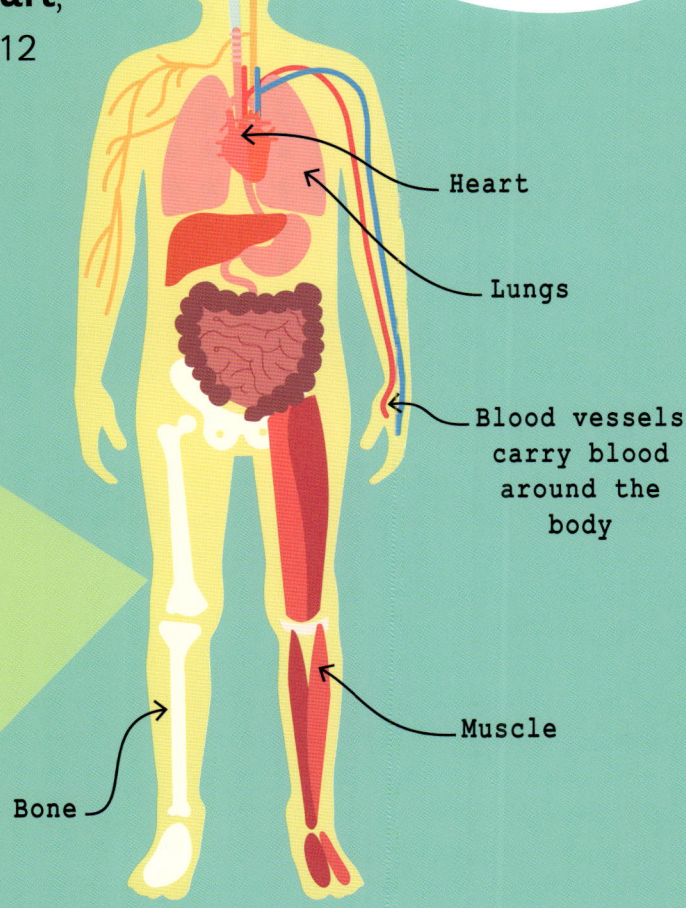

Some cells last your entire life. Others die within a day and are replaced.

- Brain
- Heart
- Lungs
- Blood vessels carry blood around the body
- Muscle
- Bone
- Bone tissue
- Muscle tissue

Only you

Cells contain your DNA – the **chemical code** that applies only to you. This is information inherited from both sides of your genetic family that makes you different from everyone else.

37 TRILLION cells inside their body.

In the genes

Genes are **instructions** in the cells (the tiniest parts of the body). They control how the body **looks**, **works**, and **grows**. They make you you!

Every person has about 20,000 different genes.

I'm a gene for red hair.

I'm a gene for brown hair.

Passing genes

Children take their genes from their **biological parents**. This is why people often **look similar** to one or both of their genetic parents. People can also inherit talents and other things from their biological family.

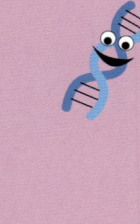

The science of studying genes is called GENETICS.

Why does my brother have red hair and I have brown hair?

Why do I look like me?

You will **be unique** even if you have brothers and sisters from the same parents. Each time parents pass on their genetic information, it will combine in different ways.

Jumping genes

American scientist **Barbara McClintock** was **studying corn** when she noticed that the colours changed over the generations. A colour would appear in one generation, then it would disappear for a while, only to happen again a few generations later. This is known as **jumping genes**, and it can **happen in humans**, too.

Grandmother
Curly hair, needs glasses

Father
Straight hair, no glasses

Child
Curly hair, needs glasses

Discovering DNA

DNA (deoxyribonucleic acid) is a chemical that carries a **set of instructions** for how the body develops. It is found inside cells, the smallest parts of the body.

DNA remains in bones and teeth for thousands of years. Scientists can study old remains to understand more about the person when they were alive.

Gene

DNA details
Each **section of DNA** is called a **gene**. Genes are the body information that affect how an organism (living thing) looks and grows.

DNA is made up of two entwined chemical strands. Viewed under a microscope, DNA looks rather like a twisted ladder.

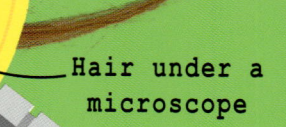

Hair under a microscope

Scene of the crime
It is possible to identify people by their DNA because it is almost **always unique**. Criminals who leave behind hair at a crime scene can be identified by the **DNA traces** in the hair.

All living things have DNA in their cells.

85% Mouse

80% Cow

70% Slug

This is the amount of DNA I share with all these different things...

90% Cat

Fly 60%

Your closest animal relative is the chimpanzee, with almost identical DNA to you.

Banana

50%

Chimpanzee

98%

Building a body
Scientists mapped out the genes needed to **build a person** by studying a complete DNA code of the human body. It is used to work out which parts of DNA are involved in different diseases.

Identical twins are the only people who share the same DNA. Other people have DNA unique to them.

25

We can all play

The human body can experiences difficulties or disabilities that may affect the way we learn, play, and do everyday things. Finding **new ways** to do things means we can still have fun together!

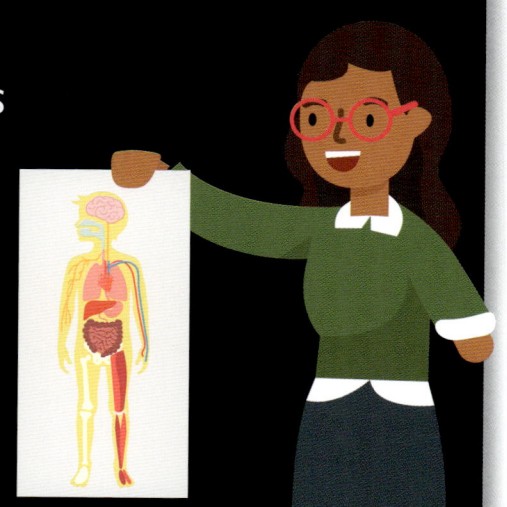

Complex bodies

Bodies are full of many complex **parts that work together**. It is possible for just about any part of the body not to work as expected. If this happens, the body may react or work in a different way to other people's.

Growing and changing

Some people have **disabilities that can make learning harder**. Sometimes the differences exist from birth, or they can develop later. They may arise from an illness or an injury. Some difficulties don't happen all the time, but come and go depending on the situation.

On the outside
All children are different, including you! Some people wear glasses to help them see. Others use wheelchairs to help them move. You **can see these differences**, so it's easier to understand them.

On the inside
There are also many **differences that cannot be seen**, so they can be harder to understand. Someone may have a difficulty that makes it hard for them to read. Tummy aches can't be seen either, but they can still affect your ability to do everyday things.

No matter what is going on with our bodies – inside or outside – we're all people who can be kind to each other and find ways to have fun together.

Try changing the rules of your favourite game so everyone can join in.

Extra help
Some children at school need more help from adults during class. You can also help by thinking of ways that we can all play the same games together. Sometimes all we need to do is to think of **a few small changes** to the rules so that everyone can join in.

Special skills
What's your talent? You might be brilliant at drawing, football, or listening. We all have things we are good at, as well as things we find hard. Talking about what we find easy or hard can be a great way to get to know each other better.

Growing up

The human body goes on an amazing journey through different **stages of life**. It's the trip of a lifetime!

Before birth
A baby can form and grow inside the uterus, one of the female reproductive organs. The uterus provides food and oxygen for the baby until it is ready to be born, usually at about nine months.

People grow the most in adolescence – up to 10 cm (4 in)!

Baby
The baby is born entirely dependent on its parent, or parents.

Toddler
Children aged two to three years are very active. Their brains are developing so they can explore the world.

Childhood
Children are now learning and growing really quickly. Their milk teeth are gradually replaced by adult teeth.

Adolescence
This is when puberty starts. The body goes through growth spurts and other changes to become more like an adult.

Young adults are usually at the peak of their physical fitness.

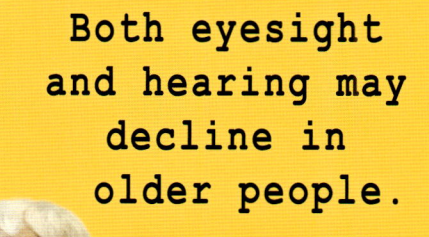

Both eyesight and hearing may decline in older people.

Young adulthood

Middle age

Old age

This stage often involves more independence. By now, many people no longer rely so heavily on family members. They usually get a job and earn their own money.

From around 40 years onwards, the skin loses its smooth surface, and wrinkles form. Muscles start to slowly weaken unless exercised properly, and the bones get weaker.

By 70, the body is more fragile. The spine shrinks, so people get shorter. Skin can bruise and bones can break more easily. The brain is not as good at remembering, so people may become forgetful.

Golden oldies

Research has shown that a healthy lifestyle can help you **live longer**. Even though parts of the body start to decline in older age, people can still lead active lives. **Aged 102**, British farmer **Fauja Singh** ran 42 km (26 miles) to complete a marathon in 2013.

Helpful hormones

Hormones are **chemical messengers** produced all over the body. They only exist in small amounts, but they affect and **manage** hundreds of **body processes**, from how we process food to how we grow.

I'm helping cells use blood sugar to make energy.

Hormone highway

Full body system
The body's endocrine system is made up of groups of cells, called **glands**, in different parts of the body. Each gland produces its own hormones. The hormones travel around the **bloodstream** and target a body part that they help to change or develop.

I'm helping the body decide what to do when it is stressed and scared.

Balancing act
Sometimes a body may create too many or too few hormones, which can cause different **effects on the body**. Medicine can be taken to **balance** the hormones.

When hormones target cells and trigger changes, they can affect a person's mood, too. Some hormones make teenagers have mood swings and feel more extreme emotions.

Gland guide

Most hormones are produced from glands in the **brain**, **neck**, and **tummy**. These glands **release hormones** if they are given a trigger, such as a change or signal in the body.

Pineal gland
Makes hormones to help the sleep cycle.

Pituitary gland
Sometimes called the master gland, it helps control other glands.

Thyroid gland
Releases hormones to control the body's metabolism (the speed that cells use oxygen).

Heart
Produces hormones to control blood pressure.

Pancreas
Makes hormones to maintain sugar levels in the blood.

Stomach and intestines
Release hormones to tell the body when it needs food, and to help digest food.

Adrenal glands
Make hormones to maintain blood pressure and prepare the body when something scary happens.

Labels on body diagram: Pineal gland, Brain, Pituitary gland, Thyroid gland, Heart, Adrenal gland, Stomach, Pancreas, Intestines

31

How long can I live?

No one knows exactly how long they will live, but thanks to **developments in medicine** and **healthier** lifestyles, many people are living longer than ever before.

70 years

Longer lives
The average age a person will live to is **70 years old**. About 200 years ago, half of newborns lived to only five years old. Today more than **97 per cent** live beyond five years old.

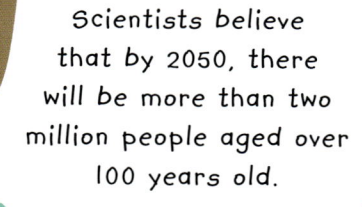

Scientists believe that by 2050, there will be more than two million people aged over 100 years old.

Good life
People are **living longer** compared to populations in the past because we have safer drinking water, better food, safer homes, and better medical care.

You could increase your chances of living longer by maintaining a healthy diet, doing regular exercise, and having plenty of sleep. Doctors also advise keeping calm and avoiding stress.

Some members of the animal kingdom live for hundreds or thousands of years!

507 years
The ocean quahog clam is the longest-living creature.

11,000 years
The ancient underwater sponge is the longest-living thing.

200 years
The bowhead whale is the longest-living mammal.

392 years
The greenland shark is the longest-living animal with a spine.

1 day
The mayfly lives for the shortest time – only a single day!

Big birthday
Jeanne Calment from France holds the record for being the oldest person ever. She lived for **122 years** and 164 days.

Most creatures get bigger as they grow up, but the paradoxical frog gets smaller! It's bigger as a tadpole than when it is a fully mature frog.

33

Uniquely human

The **animal kingdom** is full of weird and wonderful creatures with special senses and skills that humans don't have. However, there are things that **only human bodies can do**, too!

All change

All animals **adapt** over generations to suit their surroundings. **Birds** developed feathered wings for flying, or webbed feet for swimming. **Humans** also have some adaptations that other animals don't have.

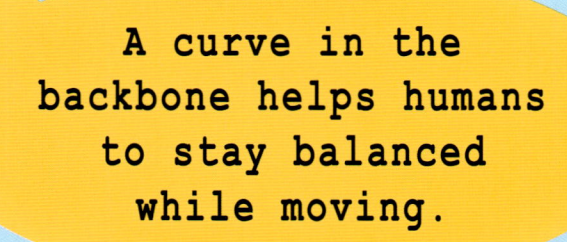

A curve in the backbone helps humans to stay balanced while moving.

Human thumbs can grasp and move more easily and freely than other animals' thumbs.

Humans can find imaginative and inventive solutions to problems due to our big brains!

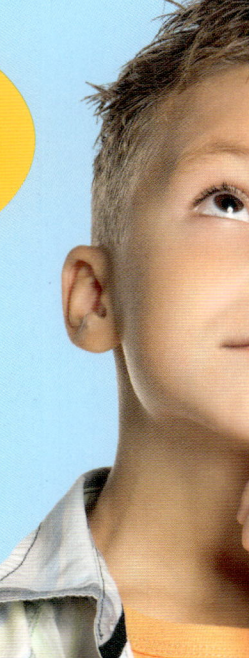

Forever young

Many animals learn **survival skills** from birth, such as finding food without help. But **human babies** are very dependent on others. A human brain is considered **fully developed** at around 25 years old.

Newborn animals can often run straight away to escape predators.

Write it down

Many animals **communicate** with their voices or with body language. Only humans can communicate through **writing in a shared language**.

Liftoff!

Many creatures only leave home to find food, shelter, or warmer weather. Humans have **bigger brains** than most animals. They have been able to invent **technology** to travel all over the world and **blast off into space**!

This crow has made a hook out of a stick to catch insects!

People once thought that humans were the only animal to make tools. But many animals, such as monkeys, otters, and crows, use tools to find or open food.

Ultimate survivors

The body can't survive for long without **essentials** like **water**, **food**, and **sleep**. But some people have pushed themselves to their **limits** – and beyond!

Without water

The body can only survive for a few days without water. In 1979, **Andreas Mihavecz** broke records, surviving **for 18 days**. He was put in jail by mistake, and the police forgot to bring him water.

I can only last for a few days without pizza!

Without food

Angus Barbieri lived on water, tea, coffee, and vitamins for more than a year, but no solid food. From 1965 he survived **for 382 days** without food and lost 133 kg (293 lb).

Without oxygen

Freediving is when divers hold their breath underwater without breathing apparatus. In 2012, **Stig Severinsen** held his breath for **22 minutes**.

Without gravity

In 1995, cosmonaut **Valeri Polyakov lived in space for 437 days**. This is the world record for the longest time anyone has survived without gravity.

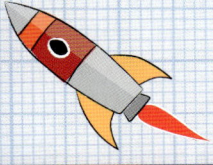

Warning!
Don't try breaking any of these records at home. They can **harm the body** and lead to lasting health problems.

Without sleep

In 1965, teenager **Randy Gardner stayed awake for 11 days**. However, he experienced slurred speech, mood swings, and memory loss afterwards.

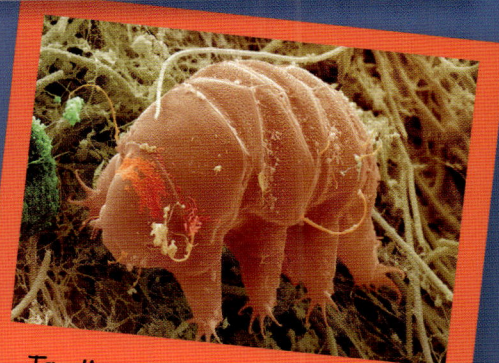

Tardigrades are only the size of a full stop, but they're the champions of survival. They can exist in boiling heat or freezing cold, and they can live for 10 years without water. They can even survive in space!

Get your facts right

Lots of countries have **funny sayings** about the human body. But are they true? Let's **separate fact from fiction**...

An apple a day keeps the doctor away.
Studies have found that people who eat more apples go to the doctor less. However, the **best diets** include lots of **different** fruits and vegetables.

TRUE

Spinach gives you muscles.
Spinach is full of vitamins, but any **leafy vegetables** can make you strong and keep your brain and heart healthy.

TRUE

If you have curly hair, it means at least one of your biological parents has passed on the curly gene.

Crusts make your hair curl.
Your hair won't look any different whether you eat your crusts or not. But **wasting food** is bad for the environment, so tuck in!

FALSE

If you swallow an apple pip, a tree will grow inside your tummy.

Don't worry! There is **no sunshine** in your tummy and **stomach acid** is far too strong for a tree to grow. Phew!

FALSE

We use 10 per cent of our brains.

False! Brain scanners have shown that **all the areas** of the brain are used. Many parts work at the same time.

FALSE

Carrots can help you see in the dark.

Crunch those carrots because there is some truth here. **Vitamin A** in carrots helps to keep the eyes **healthy** and can improve night vision.

TRUE

People catch colds from feeling cold.

Chilly air can make noses run, but a **cold virus** is the only thing that can truly cause a cold.

FALSE

Don't believe everything you hear!

39

The body's framework

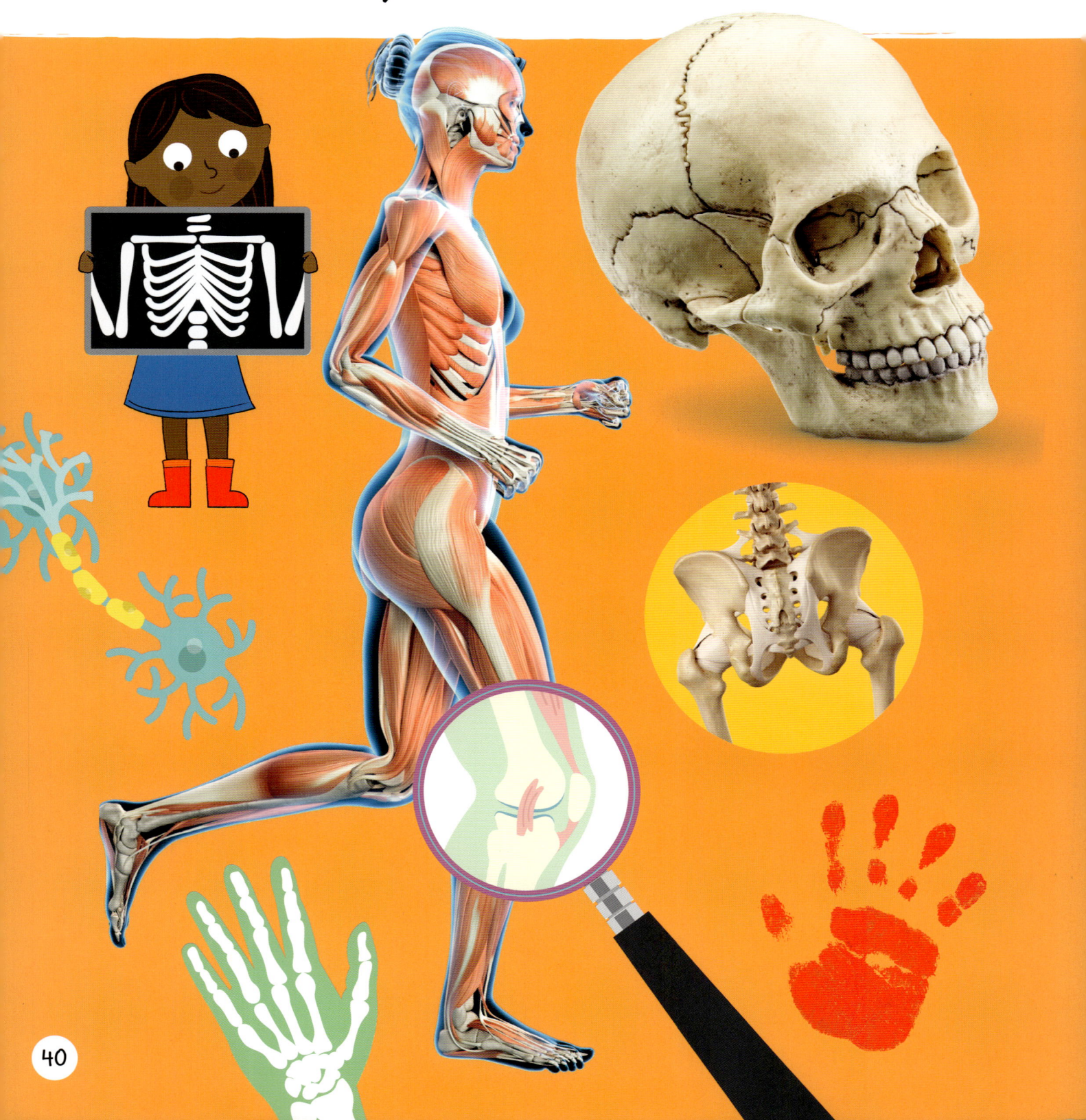

Lots of body parts are soft and squishy, so what stops you looking like a wibbly-wobbly jelly? It's the **skeleton**! Without this super strong framework, your body would collapse in a heap on the floor! Bones maintain the body's **shape**, **protect** the important parts on the inside, and team up with muscles to make the body **move**.

Extraordinary X-rays

The discovery of **invisible X-rays** by Wilhelm Röntgen **revealed** the bones of the body in a whole new light.

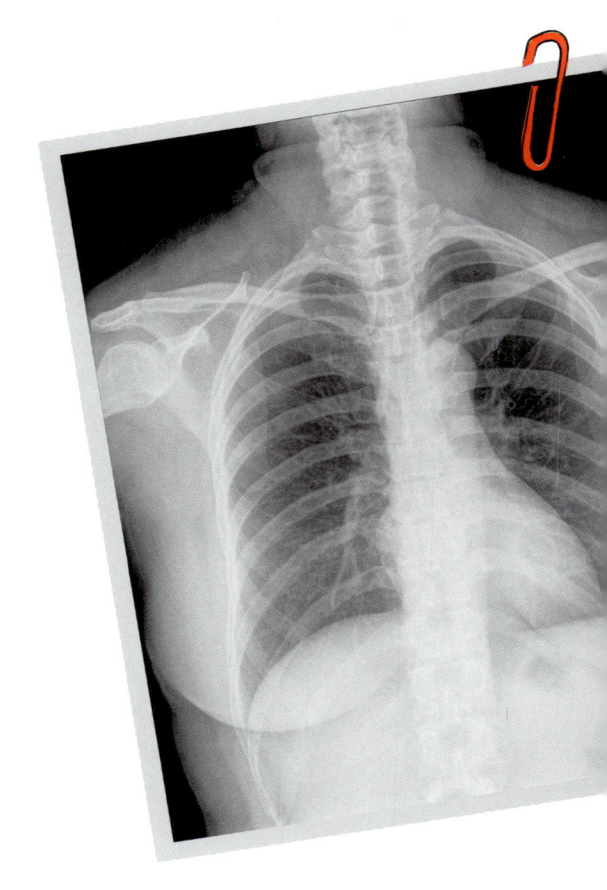

> Röntgen was awarded the Nobel Prize for Physics for his discovery.

Green light

In 1895, German physicist **Wilhelm Röntgen** was busy researching light rays when he spotted a mysterious **green light** on some of his equipment. This turned out to be **invisible light rays** he called "**X-rays**".

Medical marvel

The discovery of X-rays was an important moment in medical science. It allowed doctors to find **breaks in bones**, and for dentists to spot **problems in teeth**. Now, more than three billion medical X-rays are taken each year.

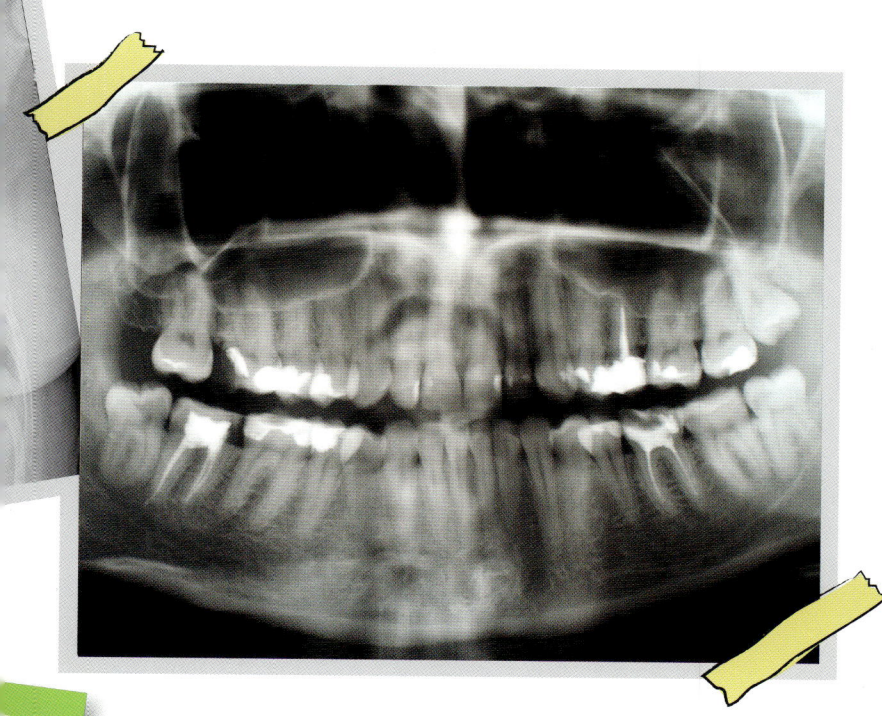

Handy work

Röntgen found that X-rays could be **beamed** through skin to show the **bones** of the body on **photographic film**. He took the first ever X-ray image of his wife's hand. The picture showed her bones and her **wedding ring**!

How X-rays work

X-rays travel through the body's soft tissues, but they get stopped by hard parts. Bones and teeth are the hardest parts in the body, so they show up where the rays become blocked.

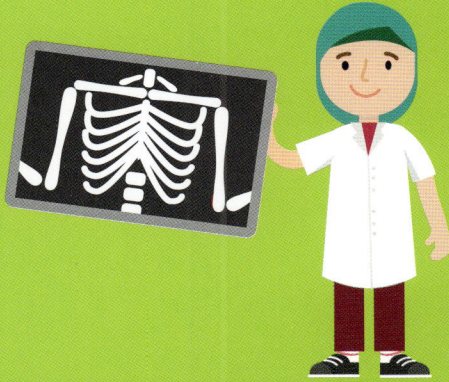

The darkest parts of the image are where the X-rays don't get stopped by something hard. The images of the bones and teeth can then be projected onto film for doctors to examine.

X-ray fish

This little fish from South America looks like it is permanently under an X-ray machine. It has see-through skin that shows its bony skeleton. This helps it to swim without being spotted by bigger, hungrier fish!

Super skeleton

The skeleton **supports** and **shapes** the entire body. It creates a strong frame, protects vital organs, and works with muscles to help the body move.

Here are some of the biggest bones in the skeleton.

- Skull
- Jawbone
- Collar bone
- Shoulder blade
- Breast bone
- Elbow joint
- Ribs
- Vertebrae (back bones)
- Pelvis
- Wrist bones
- Coccyx (tail bone)
- Finger bones
- Femur (thigh bone)
- Patella (knee cap)
- Tibia (shin bone)
- Fibula
- Ankle joints
- Foot bones

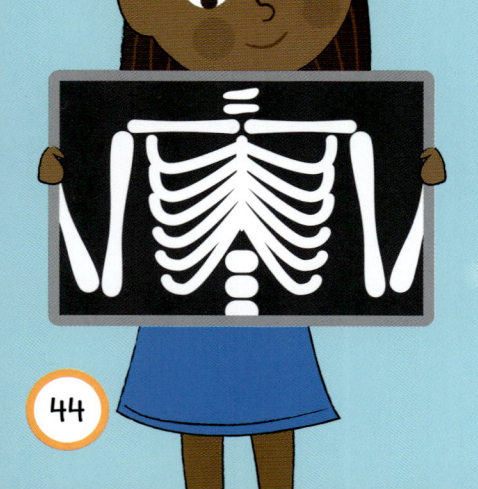

In total, you have 206 bones. They make up 15 per cent of your weight.

44

Endoskeletons

An endoskeleton is **inside the body**. Mammals, reptiles, birds, and fish have endoskeletons. Most are made of hard bone, but sharks and rays have endoskeletons made of softer cartilage.

Endoskeletons grow as the animal grows.

Giraffe

Elephant

Exoskeletons

Exoskeletons are hard coverings on the **outside of the body**. They are made of minerals and proteins that are strong but flexible. Animals with exoskeletons include ladybirds and crabs.

Ladybird

Centipede

Cockroach

Spider

Crab

Bionic bodies

People who have mobility issues can be given **artificial exoskeleton suits** to help them. These battery-powered packs can correct a person's posture and help them get moving.

Artificial exoskeletons can be made for the whole body...

...or just a single body part, such as a leg.

How tall can I grow?

Height is how tall someone is when measured **from their head to their feet**. Some families have lots of tall people, while others are of average height. Let's find out what affects your height.

Family genes
The genes inherited from *biological* parents are an important factor in a person's potential height. If the parents are tall, it's likely that the child will be tall, too.

Eat well, grow well
Eating a healthy and nutritious diet is important for good growth. The vitamins and minerals in food help bones and muscles develop. A poor diet often means a person grows more slowly.

Growing up
Feel taller in the morning? That's because you are! When a person lies down, the spine straightens, and the discs in the spine plump up to make the person taller by morning.

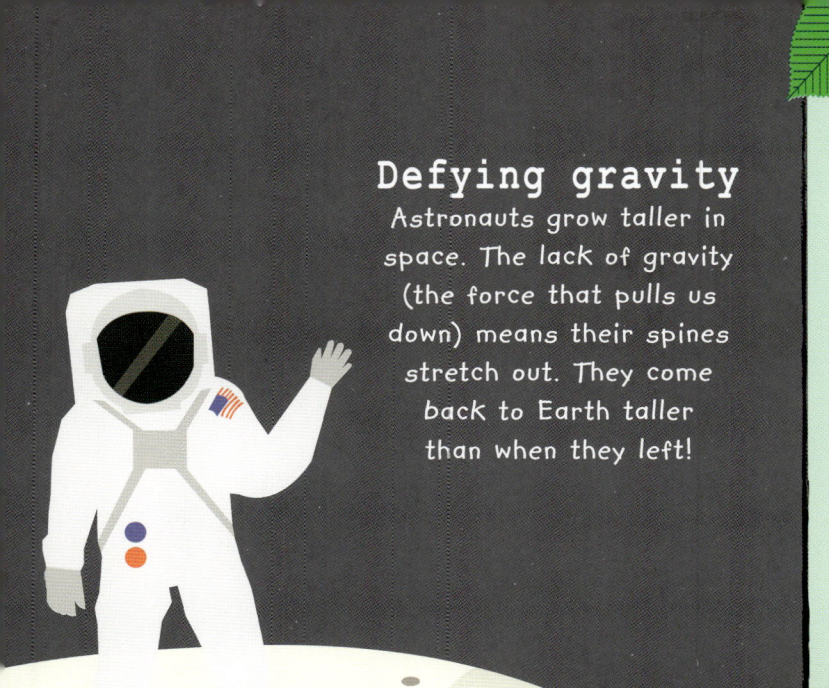

Defying gravity
Astronauts grow taller in space. The lack of gravity (the force that pulls us down) means their spines stretch out. They come back to Earth taller than when they left!

Dizzy heights
Giraffes are the tallest animals in the world. A male giraffe can grow to 5.5 metres (18 feet) – more than three times the height of an average male adult!

Gland problems
A good diet and healthy lifestyle can help someone grow to their full genetic potential. However, sometimes glands or other issues can cause a person to be particularly tall or small.

Record-breakers
Robert Wadlow (1918-1940) was the tallest person who ever lived. He was 2.7 metres (8 feet and 11 inches) tall – that's about half the height of a giraffe.

Strong skull

The skull is made up of **22 bones**. It protects the brain and sensory organs inside, such as the ears.

The skull is a bit like a jigsaw puzzle. Each piece has to come together for it to work properly.

Joining together
The bones in the **cranium** only join together when a child is about two years old. Before this, the brain has plenty of **space to grow**.

Mandible
The mandible (lower jaw) is the only bone in the skull that **can move**, allowing us to eat and speak. Ligaments, which are like straps, keep it attached to the skull.

Meninges
Between the skin and the brain are three **thin layers of tissue** called meninges (dura mater, arachnoid mater, pia mater). These help protect the brain.

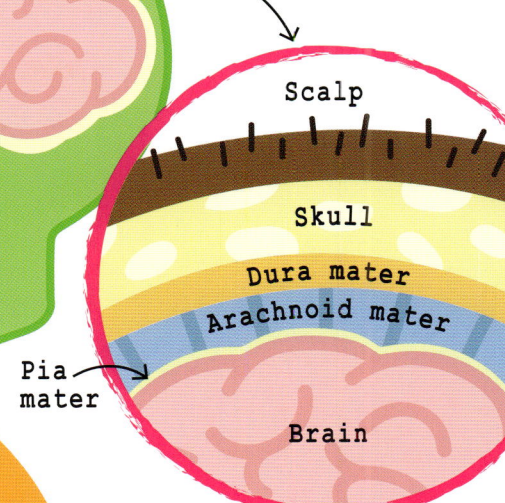

Scalp
Skull
Dura mater
Arachnoid mater
Pia mater
Brain

Cranium
The cranium is made up of eight bones that form **a helmet around the brain**. If a person bumps their head, it can protect the brain.

Pockets of air
The skull has air-filled cavities (spaces) inside it, which lie behind the cheekbones and forehead. These help **stop the skull being too heavy**.

Facial bones
Fourteen bones make up the bones of the face. They **give the face shape** and protect important structures, such as the eyes.

Brilliant bones

Bones may look solid, but they grow and change shape. This **living tissue** protects organs, supports the body's shape, and helps us move.

Bone weight
Bones make up around 15 per cent of body weight. They are made of strong fibres – called collagen – and also minerals like calcium.

What are bones made of?

Spongy bone
Spongy bone is full of holes, but it's hard, not squishy. Blood vessels and nerves travel through the holes. That's why it hurts when bones break!

Compact bone
Compact bone is found on the outside of the bone, and muscles are attached to it. It is super tough.

Red marrow
Red bone marrow is found in spongy bone. It contains stem cells that make blood.

- Red bone marrow
- Yellow bone marrow

Osteons
Inside the compact bone, special structures called osteons wrap around a hollow space in the middle where blood vessels and nerves sit.

Yellow marrow
Yellow bone marrow is made of fat cells. Children have red marrow until they are seven, then it starts to get replaced by yellow marrow.

Bone growth
Having differences in our bones is normal. It is possible for bones to grow differently to the standard shapes.

Hipbone

Femur

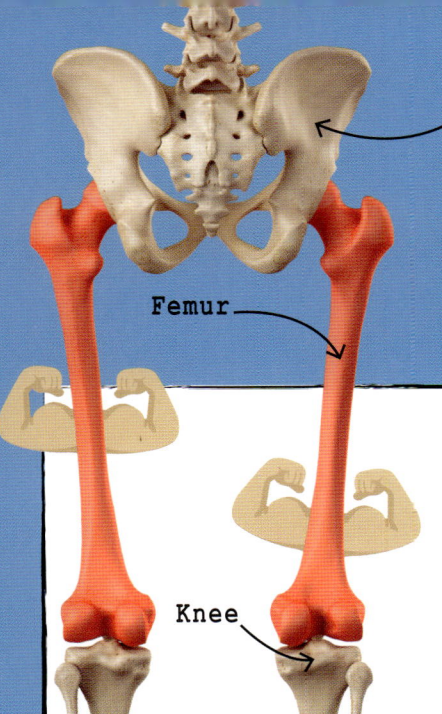

Knee

Bone up on these facts...

Strongest bone

The femur (thigh bone) is the strongest and longest bone in the human body. It joins the hip and knee.

The funny bone isn't a bone! It's a nerve that runs close to the bone. When you bang it, it hurts!

Ulnar nerve (funny bone)

Ouch!

How many?

Babies are born with 300 bones, but adults have 206 bones. Many bones join together after the baby is born. The coccyx (tail bone) starts off as up to 5 separate bones that fuse into one over time!

Important bones

The bones making up the spine are strongly linked together, but still allow the body to bend in different directions. These bones protect the spinal cord, which connects the brain to the rest of the body.

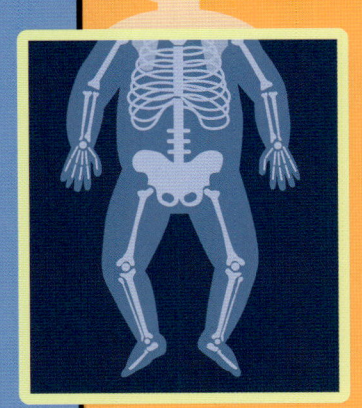

Spine

Spinal cord

More than half the body's bones are in the hands and feet.

51

Tough tissues

Cells are the **smallest structures** in the body. They can't be seen with the naked eye, but they **join together** to form the **tissues** that can be seen.

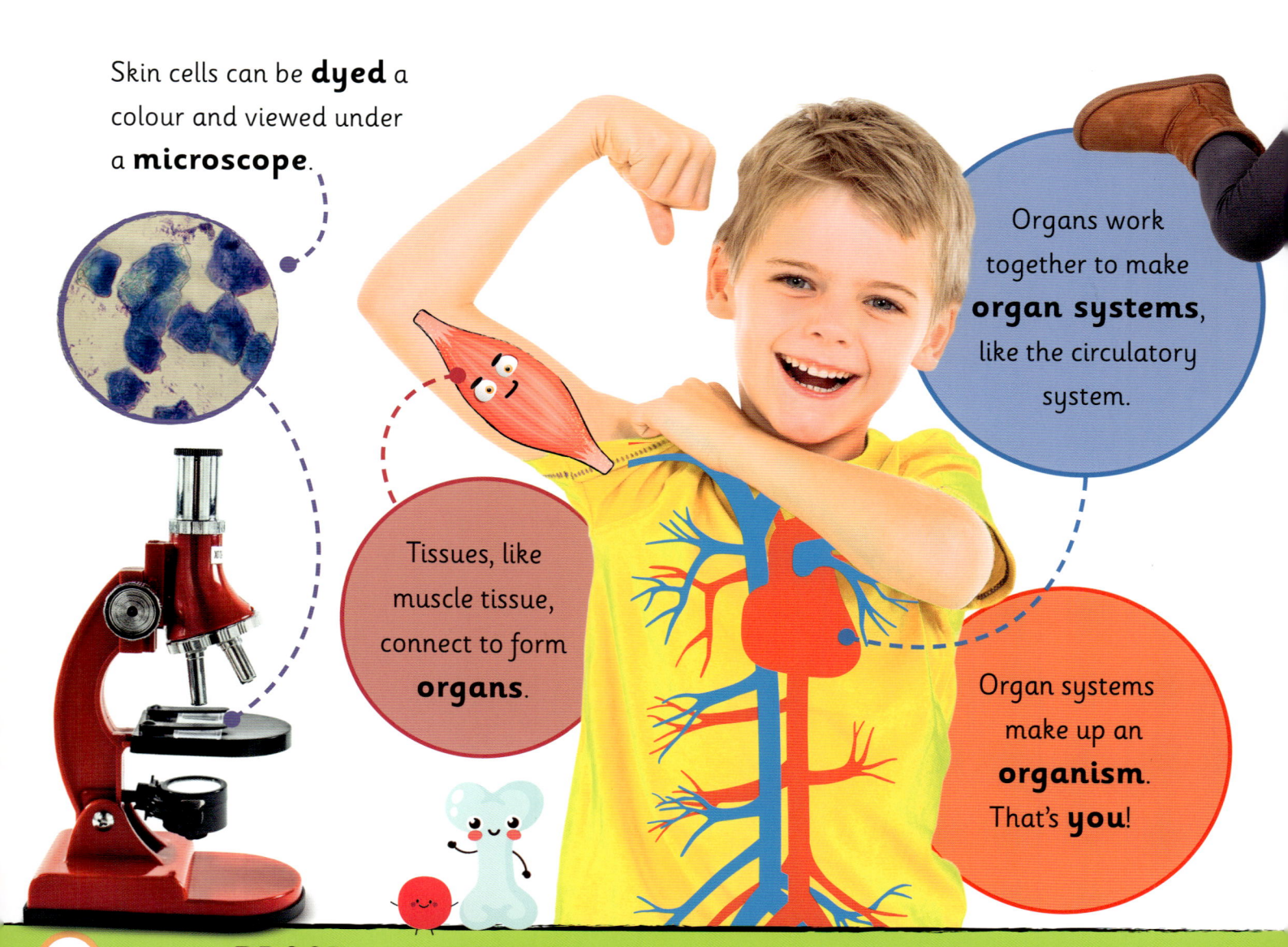

Skin cells can be **dyed** a colour and viewed under a **microscope**.

Tissues, like muscle tissue, connect to form **organs**.

Organs work together to make **organ systems**, like the circulatory system.

Organ systems make up an **organism**. That's **you**!

BLOOD and BONES are also types of tissues.

Tissue types

There are four basic types of tissues.

Muscle tissue

Muscle tissue is one of the four basic body tissues. Muscles contract – get shorter – to cause movement. Skipping, jumping, and sitting are possible because of muscle tissue.

Nervous tissue

This is another basic tissue. Nerves pass on information from one part of the body to another. Information can travel from the little toe to reach the brain all because of nervous tissue.

Connective tissue

This type of tissue gives shape and support to organs. Think about skin – connective tissue here makes the skin tough and flexible so it can protect you, but still allows you to move about.

Total coverage

Epithelium tissue protects the body's surfaces and linings, such as inside the mouth and cheeks.

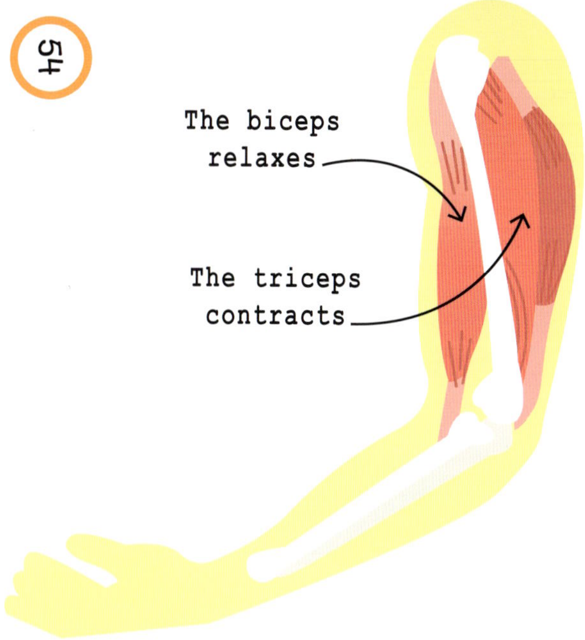

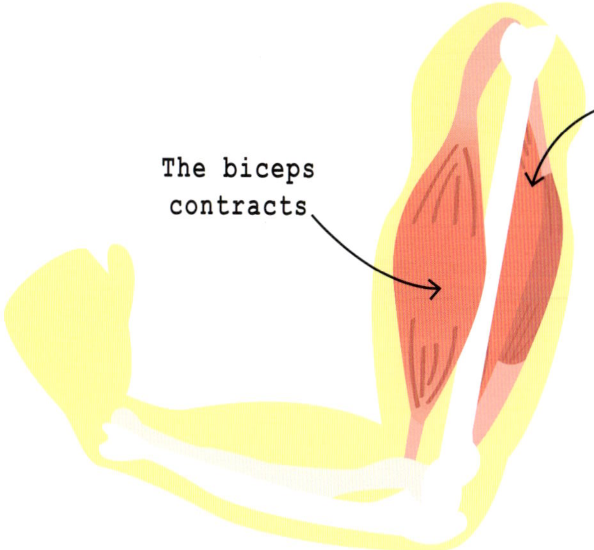

On the move

The musculoskeletal system is made of muscles and bones. **Skeletal muscle** (muscle attached to bones) causes bones to move. This is why we can **move bits of the body!**

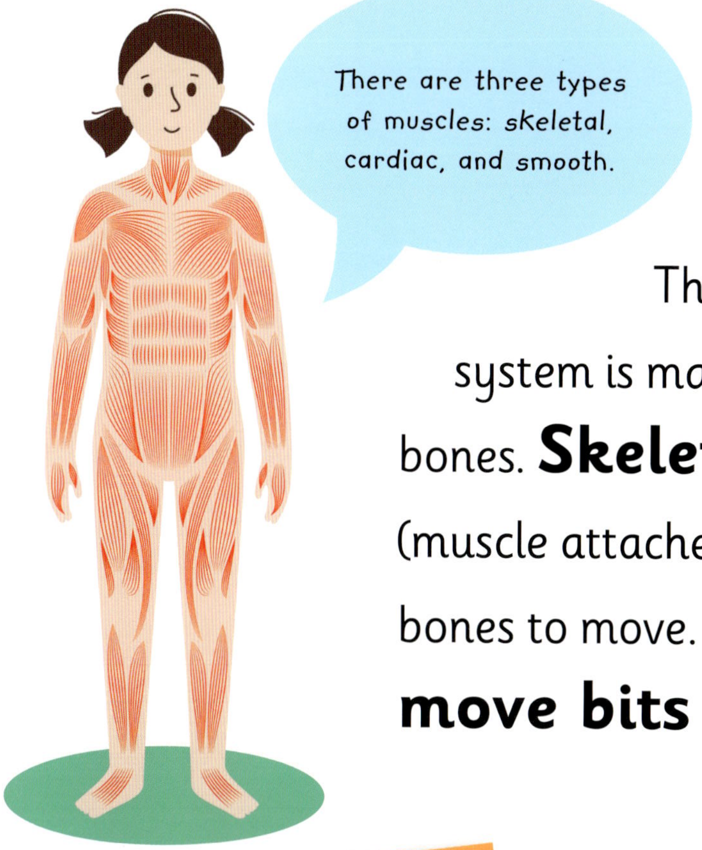

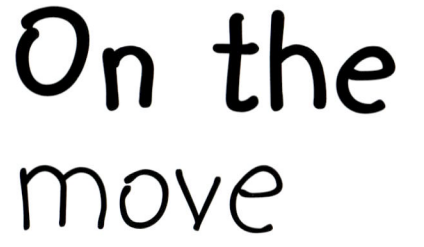

There are three types of muscles: skeletal, cardiac, and smooth.

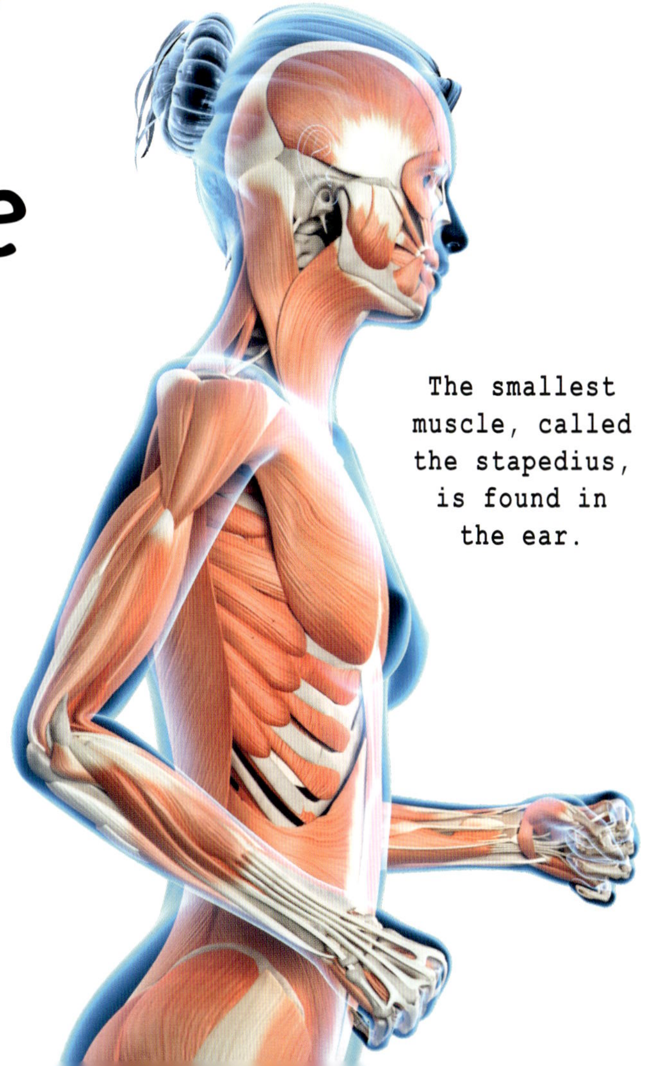

Muscle pairs

Muscles work together to cause movement. One muscle **contracts** (shortens), and the other muscle **relaxes** (lengthens).

The triceps relaxes

The biceps contracts

The biceps relaxes

The triceps contracts

The smallest muscle, called the stapedius, is found in the ear.

54

Gluteus maximus

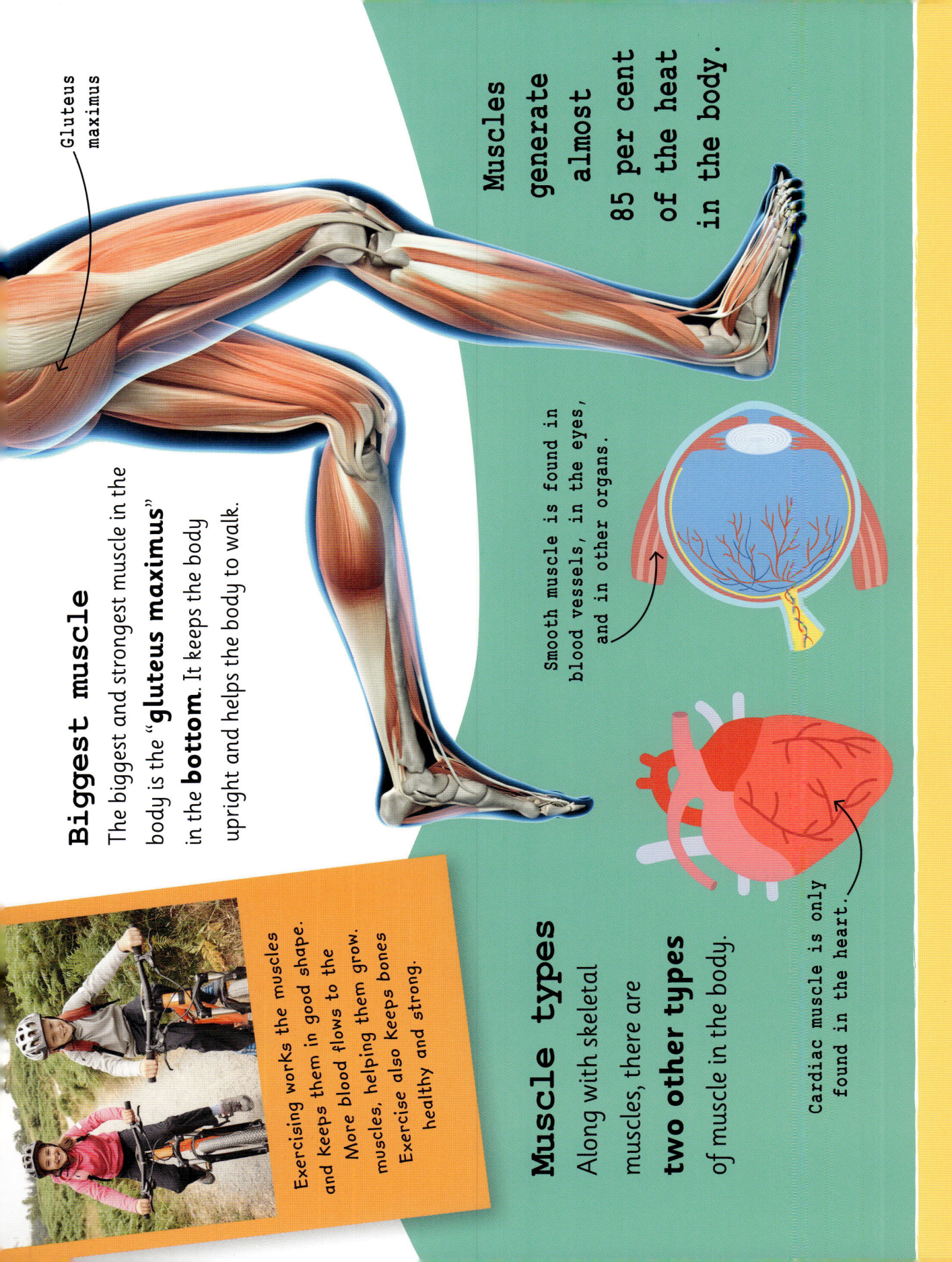

Biggest muscle

The biggest and strongest muscle in the body is the **"gluteus maximus"** in the **bottom**. It keeps the body upright and helps the body to walk.

Exercising works the muscles and keeps them in good shape. More blood flows to the muscles, helping them grow. Exercise also keeps bones healthy and strong.

Muscle types

Along with skeletal muscles, there are **two other types** of muscle in the body.

Muscles generate almost 85 per cent of the heat in the body.

Smooth muscle is found in blood vessels, in the eyes, and in other organs.

Cardiac muscle is only found in the heart.

Smooth and cardiac muscle are involuntary. This means they contract on their own WITHOUT YOU KNOWING IT!

55

How high can I jump?

Your mighty **muscles** and brilliant **bones** work together every time you move. But what kind of **heights** can the human body reach? And who are the record-breakers of the animal kingdom?

Animal antics

Animal bodies are specially adapted for their environments and lifestyles. Some jump to **move around** more freely, and others need to **pounce on prey**.

Fleas can jump 150 times their own body height — that's the same as you jumping over a 60-storey building!

German-born Rehm competes wearing a prosthetic blade.

Blade jumper
In the long jump, competitors take a running start then jump as far as possible, landing in a sand pit. In 2021, Markus Rehm set the Paralympian world record of 8.6 m (28 ft).

Aiming high
In the high jump, athletes take a running jump and leap over a high bar. Cuba's Javier Sotomayor set the record in 1993 when he jumped 2.45 m (8 ft).

Sotomayor's record breaking leap is eight times higher than most people can jump!

Dolphins jump clean out of the water, reaching heights of more than 7 m (25 ft). They do this to see what is happening above the water, and to look for prey on the surface.

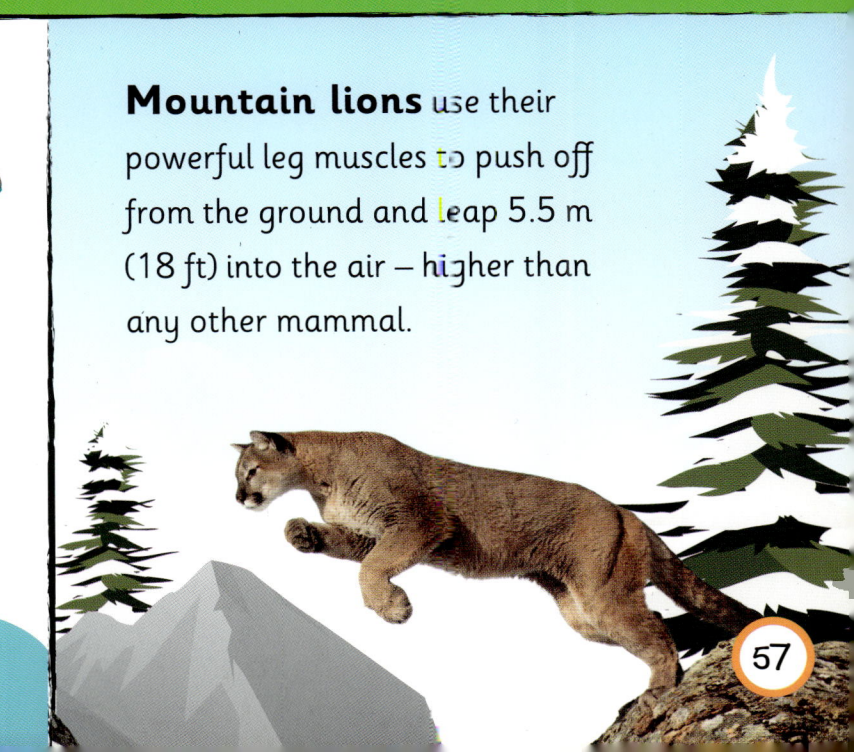

Mountain lions use their powerful leg muscles to push off from the ground and leap 5.5 m (18 ft) into the air – higher than any other mammal.

Nerves of steel

The **nervous system** helps parts of the body to **communicate** with each other.

It reacts to changes outside and inside the body.

Left and right
The **left side** of the brain controls the right side of the body. The **right side** of the brain controls the left side of the body. This complex arrangement works well!

Speedy messengers
Some information travels in the nervous system **as fast as a racing car**! The thicker the nerve, the faster the information can travel.

Spinal cord

Nerves

Information superhighway
Threadlike structures, called nerves, **send and receive messages** between the **brain** and the **body**. Most information goes through the spinal cord first, which is the main "motorway" to the brain.

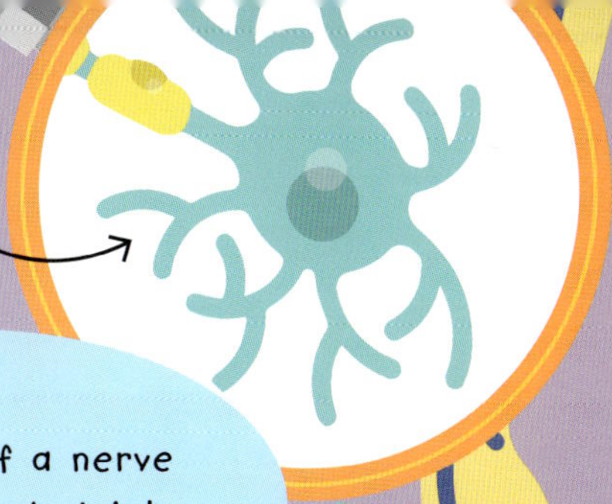

What do you prefer?

The activities we find calming could be **directed by the nervous system**. Some people find it calms their nerves to move about, such as jumping or running. Others find that going somewhere quiet and cosy and being still is more calming.

Nerve cell

The shape of a nerve depends on what job it is doing

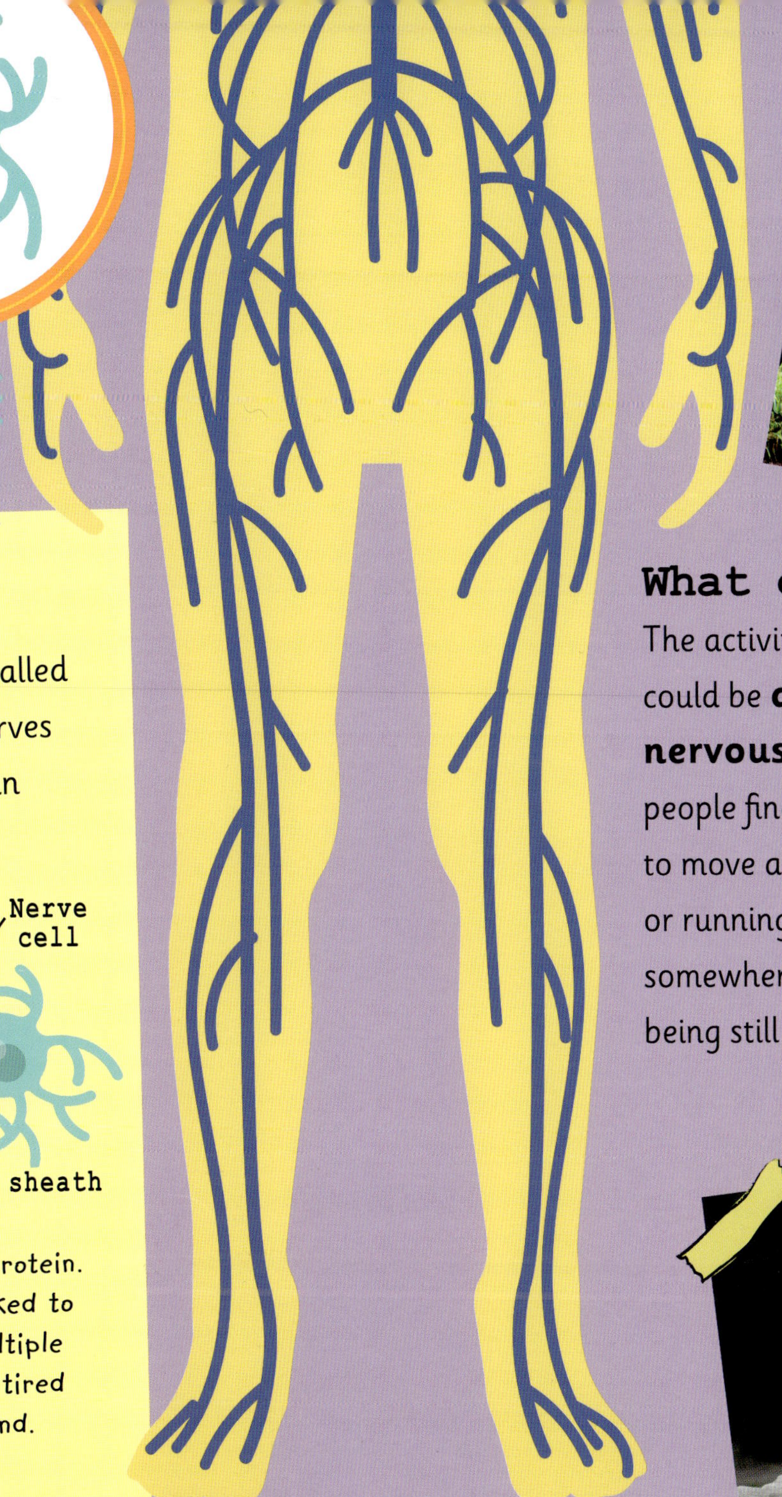

Myelin power

Some nerves have a covering, called **a myelin sheath**. These nerves transmit information faster than nerves without a covering.

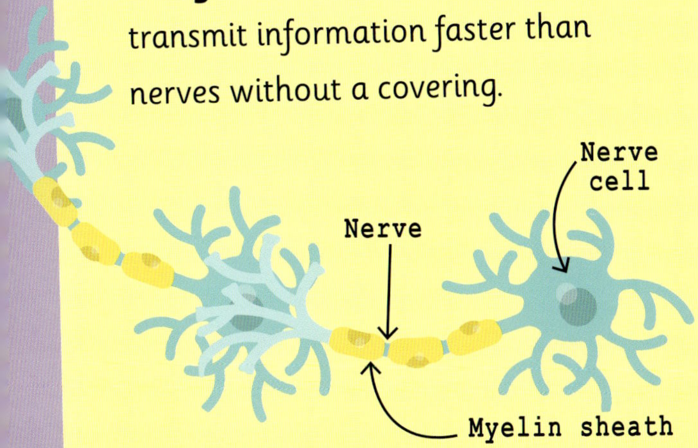

Nerve cell

Myelin sheath

Nerve

Myelin is made up of fats and protein. Some medical problems are linked to issues with myelin, such as multiple sclerosis, which makes people tired or have trouble getting around.

59

Reflex actions

Reflexes are actions we do **without even thinking** about them. They are the body's way of protecting itself. The action happens before you can even think about it!

On average, a person blinks

Typical response
Sneezing happens when something has **irritated the lining of the nose**. Droplets come out of the nose and mouth and can travel quite a distance!

Achooo!

Auto-pilot
Reflexes are **automatic**. They skip past the brain so the response can happen quickly to keep the body safe. Signals go through the spinal cord and the brain is told about them later.

What's up, doc?
Doctors will check some reflexes to make sure they are working. By **tapping the knee** with a tendon hammer, they can check the receptors, nerves, and muscles.

Second nature
The body performs lots of reflex actions every day, like **blinking**, **yawning**, and **sneezing**. These protect parts of the body, such as the eyes, and they are automatic – you can't stop them from happening!

Achooo!

15–20 TIMES A MINUTE.

From day one
A baby has in-built **reflexes for survival**. They automatically know how to suck milk, and, when someone strokes their palm, they will grasp the finger.

Survival of the fittest
Many baby animals can **walk right after being born**. To survive in the wild, they need to get up and move as soon as possible.

Strong signal
Touching something hot turns on sense receptors in the finger. **Receptors** are part of the nervous system. They **send a signal** to the spinal cord that tells the arm muscle to move away from the hot object.

61

Humerus

Radius

Ulna

Femur

Kneecap

Tibia

Fibula

The limbs

The limbs (**arms** and **legs**) help the body move. The bones here are among the longest and strongest.

An arm and a leg

Each arm and leg has long bones with a **hinge-like joint** to bend the limb. In the arm, the humerus links by the elbow to the radius and ulna. In the leg, the femur links by the knee to the tibia and fibula.

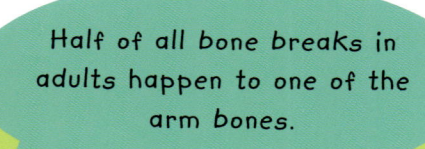

Half of all bone breaks in adults happen to one of the arm bones.

Our different bodies

Not everyone has arms and legs that **work the same way**. A person may have been injured or the brain may not send and receive **messages** across the body. Arms and legs may develop differently, too.

If the bones in the body were COMPLETELY SOLID,

Lightweight legs

For many people, the legs **support the weight** of the torso (the part of the body between the shoulders and pelvis). The legs move the body, so bones are a bit **bendy** and have a mesh-like structure inside them.

For Paralympic athletes who have a missing leg or legs, running blades are used to compete in races. These strong yet lightweight prosthetic (artificial) limbs are tailor-made to suit the individual.

Working in pairs

Walking and running usually involves the limbs working together. The legs and feet **carry the body along**, and the arms **move along in time**. This helps the person balance and pick up speed.

it wouldn't be easy to lift them.

Getting around

People with mobility issues may sometimes use aids, such as **crutches**, **sticks**, or **wheelchairs**. Some wheelchairs are powered by the user's arms moving the wheels. Motorized wheelchairs use batteries and are controlled by a joystick.

63

Cartilage that coats the joints is at least twice as slippery as ice.

Joining in

Every bendy bit of the body contains a joint — and there are hundreds of them! Without these **flexible links** between bones, the skeleton would be stuck still like a statue and couldn't move.

Joining the joints

Here are the **structures** that help make up a moving **joint**.

Tendons
Tissues shaped like ropes that join muscles to bone.

Cartilage
Tough tissue that protects the bone and allows smooth movement at the joints.

Synovial fluid
Fluid that fills the space inside the joint to help the bones move more easily.

Ligaments
Strong bands of tissue that hold the bones together.

Binding bones

The joints in the body lie where two bones meet, and help to bind the bones together. Most **joints move freely** and easily, such as in the knees and elbows. Others **fuse the bones** together, such as the ones in the skull.

The knees are the largest joints in the human body.

64

Smooth movers

Joints that move are called synovial joints. Each type of **joint moves in a different way**, and some body parts have multiple joints working together. Here are some examples of different types of joints.

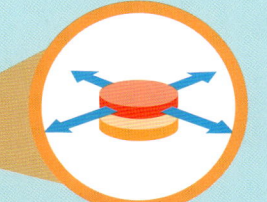

Plane/gliding joint
Two flattened bones slide over one another.

Pivot joint
The end of one bone swivels around another, like a steering wheel.

About 10 per cent of people are born with hypermobile joints, which can move in greater amounts. These people may be able to bend some of their body parts the wrong way because the joint is so flexible. If this is you, then avoid bending them the wrong way just to show your friends and family. You might be more likely to sprain or hurt your joints.

Ball and socket joint
The ball-shaped bone fits perfectly into the cup-shaped bone, like an egg in an egg cup. This allows movement in many directions.

The achilles tendon, attaching the calf muscle to the heel, is the strongest tendon of all and gives you a spring in your step!

Hinge joint
One bone fits into the other, like two pieces of a jigsaw. They work like the hinge of a door moving in only one direction.

65

Protective pelvis

The pelvis **connects** the spine to the legs. It is made of **bone**, with some **muscle** at the base. It has a few different jobs to do.

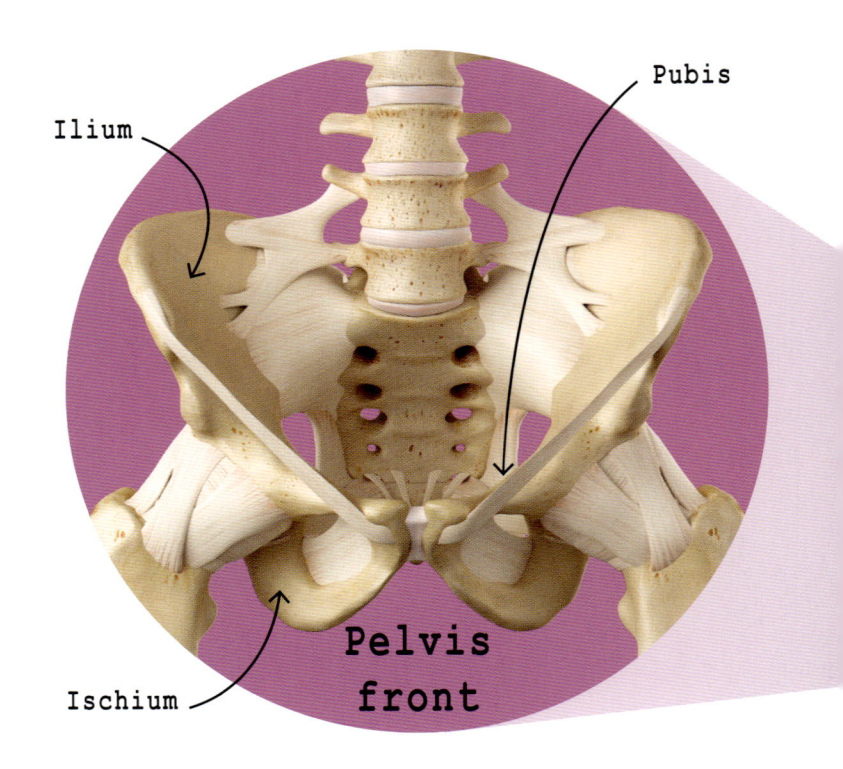

Ilium
Pubis
Ischium
Pelvis front

Bony bowl
The pelvis has **three bones** on each side (ilium, pubis, ischium), and two at the back (sacrum, coccyx).

Pregnancy
The fetus grows inside a part of the body called the **womb**. This sits inside the pelvis where it is protected. The pelvis **acts as a cradle** to hold the growing baby.

Important parts
Pelvic floor muscles, found at the bottom of the pelvis, help to **keep wee and poo inside**. These muscles relax when we get rid of waste.

What it does

The pelvis **protects some organs**. The bladder and large bowel lie within the pelvis, and the female reproductive organs are here, too.

Sacrum

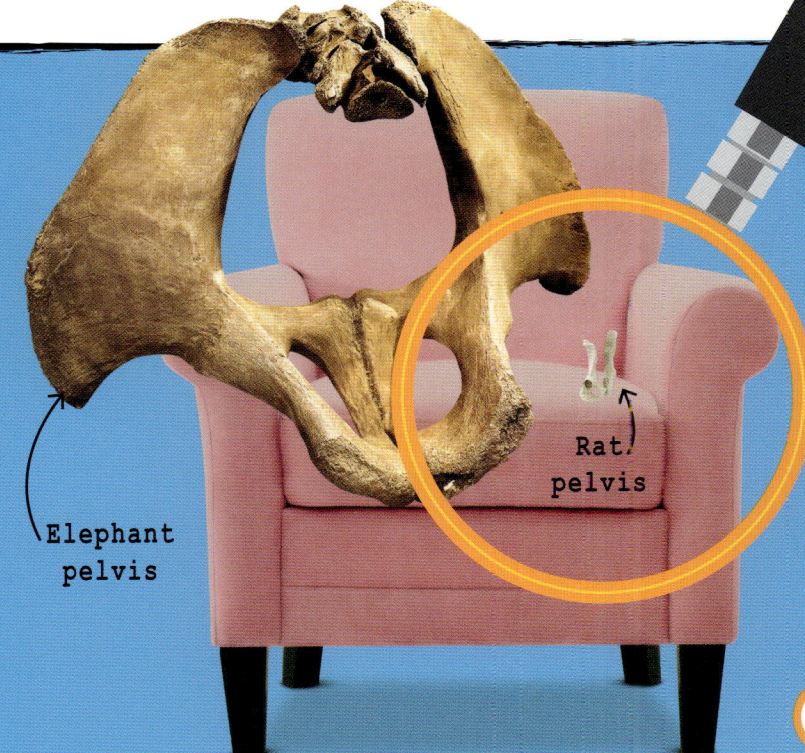

Coccyx

Pelvis back

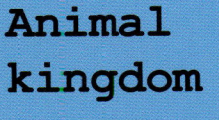

Animal kingdom

An elephant's pelvis is the **size of an armchair**! A rat's pelvis is tiny, but similar to the shape of a human pelvis.

Elephant pelvis

Rat pelvis

Coming in handy

Hands allow people to **grab** and **grasp**, **push** and **pull**, and **catch** and **carry**. You can do all kinds of things without one or both hands, too.

About one in every 500 people has an extra finger.

Thumbs up
Thumbs **move in a different way** to fingers. Each thumb can reach every finger on the same hand, which helps with lifting and handling.

More than half the bones of the body are in the hands and feet.

Hands on
Each hand has **27 bones**. There are **14 finger bones**, **5 palm bones**, and **8 wrist bones**. There is also muscle and lots of tendons (ropelike tissue that joins muscle to bone) that keep the bones moving.

Palm bones

Wrist bones

Finger bones

Have your knuckles ever made a "pop" sound? The fluid inside of the knuckle joints contains bubbles that sometimes pop when you make a big stretch or bend your fingers.

A hand lost by illness, injury, or accident can be replaced by a prosthetic (artificial) hand. Lightweight designs come with special sensory technology to detect heat, cold, and pressure.

Get a grip
Hands can grip in **two main ways**, according to the task.

Power grip
Grasping an object tightly using all the fingers and thumb is the most powerful grip. This is used to catch a ball or lift weights.

Power grip

The fingertips have more nerve endings than any other body part, so they are super sensitive to pain, heat, or cold.

Precision grip
A pinching hold between the thumb and fingertips is best for tasks involving small or delicate objects. This grip is used to hold a pen or tie shoelaces.

Precision grip

69

Hard as nails

Fingers and toes would suffer more bumps without nails to **protect the tips**. Fingernails improve the sense of touch by helping fingers to **grip**, **lift**, **open**, and **drag**.

Fingernails grow about 5 cm (2 in) a year.

Inside a nail
There is more to nails than you might realize.

The top of the nail is the hard "plate".

The root sits in the nail bed. New cells form here, then they move forwards, harden into plates, and die.

The nail bed is made up of living skin cells.

If you lose a nail, it will grow back. It takes 6 months to regrow a fingernail, and a year for a toenail.

It takes about six months for cells to move from the root to the tip.

Fingernails GROW FASTER on the hand

Neat nails

It is important to look after the nails. Keeping them **clean avoids infection**, and keeping them cut prevents **breakage or splitting**. Yellowy brown nails can be a sign of infection or an allergic reaction.

Cutting nails doesn't hurt because there are no nerve endings.

A parrot's beak, claws, and talons contain keratin.

A rhino horn is made of keratin.

Keratin

Fingers and thumbs grow about 34 m (110 ft) of nail during the average lifetime.

Tough stuff

Nails are made of a tough cell substance called **keratin**. As plates of keratin pile up, they create a **strong covering** for the fingers and toes. Keratin is also found in hair and skin, but is strongest in the nails.

Keratin kings

Keratin is an even bigger part of many **animal bodies**. It can be found in **talons**, **claws**, **scales**, **beaks**, **feathers**, and **hooves**.

My shell is also made of keratin.

you use most often!

71

Making your mark

Have you noticed the **swirly**, **whirly patterns** all over your fingertips? No one else in the world shares the same **fingerprints** as you. They are unique!

Parts of the pattern

Tiny **ridges on the fingertips** help fingers to grip. The **patterns** they make form the fingerprints. They are a combination of **arches**, **whorls**, and **loops**.

Sweaty prints
Sweat and natural oils are released from pores (holes) in the skin. They seep out from the fingertips in tiny amounts. Every time you touch something, it leaves a fingerprint impression made from the sweat and oil. Often the prints are not visible, but experts can detect them.

Arches
Visible in about 5 per cent of fingerprints

Whorls
Visible in about 35 per cent of fingerprints

Loops
Visible in about 60 per cent of fingerprints

Crime scene

Investigators can take fingerprints from a crime scene using **special powder**. They check the fingerprint against databases of fingerprints to help identify the criminal.

Leaving no trace

Some people have a genetic condition called adermatoglyphia, which means that they are **born without fingerprints**. There are only four families in the world known to have it.

Once the skin is dry, the body produces more oils and the wrinkles disappear.

Wrinkly fingers

The skin produces an **oil** to keep it clean and **waterproof**. When we stay in the water too long, the oil is washed away and the skin becomes **wrinkly**. This helps us to grip wet objects more easily.

Feet first

Feet help to **support** a person's body weight. They are also flexible enough to **keep the body balanced**.

A QUARTER of all the body's bones are

The heel is the biggest and strongest bone in the foot.

Foot formation
Each foot has **26 bones**. Seven bones form the **heel and ankle**, while five more bones make up the **middle**. The **big toe** has two bones, and the **other toes** have three bones each.

Ankle bones

Heel

When walking or running, it's mainly the front and back of the foot that take the weight and touch the ground. The arch of the foot puts a spring in the step and absorbs shocks.

...in the feet.

Smelly feet
There are half a million **sweat glands** in the feet, making them very sweaty! Foot bacteria is the same that is used to make **stinky cheeses**, which explains the strong pong!

The feet produce 0.5 litres (1 pint) of sweat each day.

Walk of life
The average person takes a whopping **150 million steps** in their entire lifetime! **Wow**!

The thickest skin is found on the soles of the feet.

Big toe

Toes

Sole of the foot

Heel

75

The making of

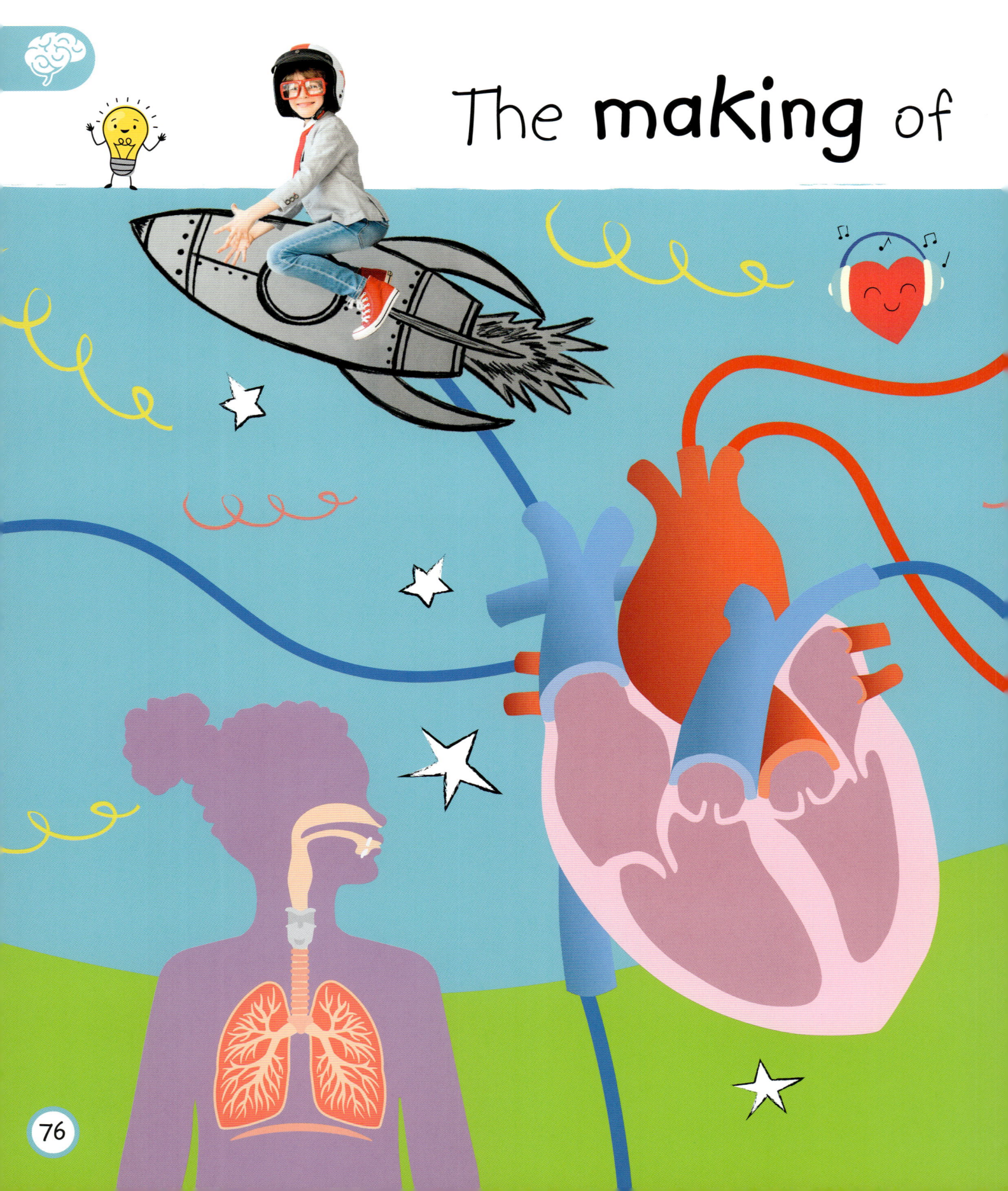

me

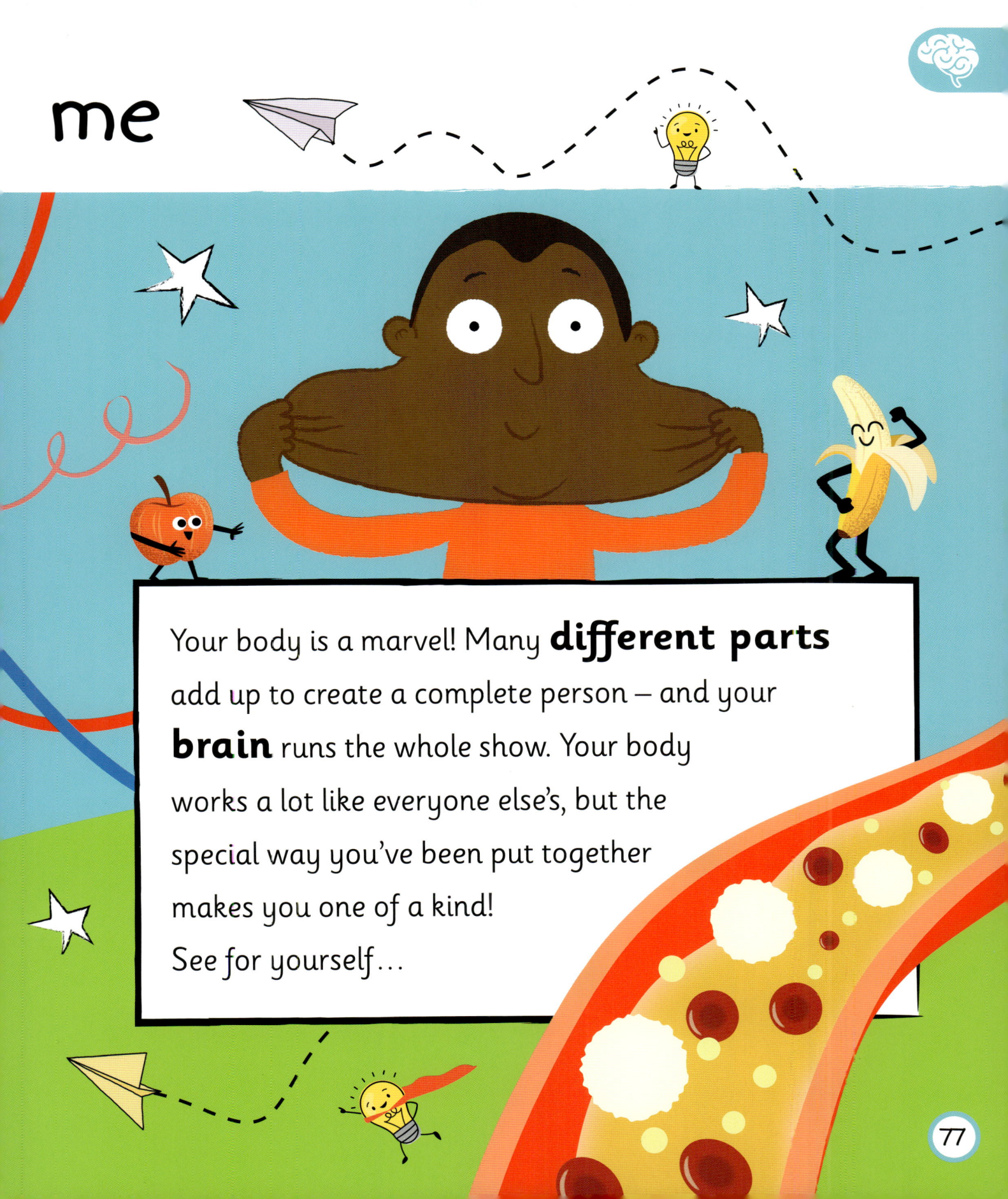

Your body is a marvel! Many **different parts** add up to create a complete person – and your **brain** runs the whole show. Your body works a lot like everyone else's, but the special way you've been put together makes you one of a kind!
See for yourself…

Baby's beginning

Babies are **bundles of joy**! But how do they grow? And what is life like for the baby before birth?

Safe place
A baby grows **inside a womb** – an organ that protects the baby during pregnancy. The womb keeps the baby **safe and warm**, and stretches as the baby grows bigger.

At least 350,000 babies are born EVERY DAY.

Pregnancy lasts for about nine months.

In the womb
The baby doesn't need to breathe or eat food because they get **oxygen** and **nutrients** through the placenta and umbilical cord.

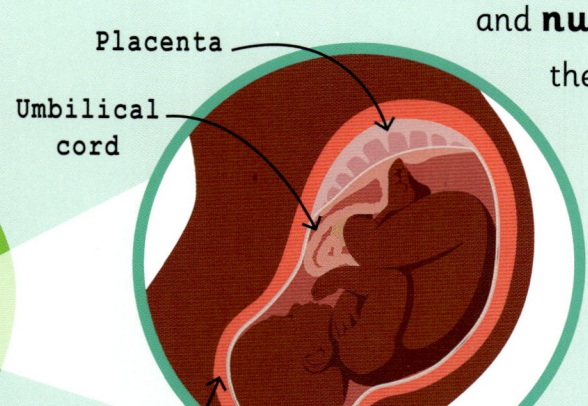

Placenta
Umbilical cord
Womb

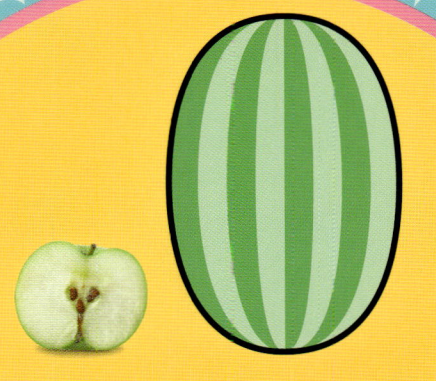

Bigger and bigger

During a pregnancy, the baby grows from the size of a **tiny apple pip** to the size of a **watermelon**! The growing baby is seen on the outside as the visible "bump" of a tummy.

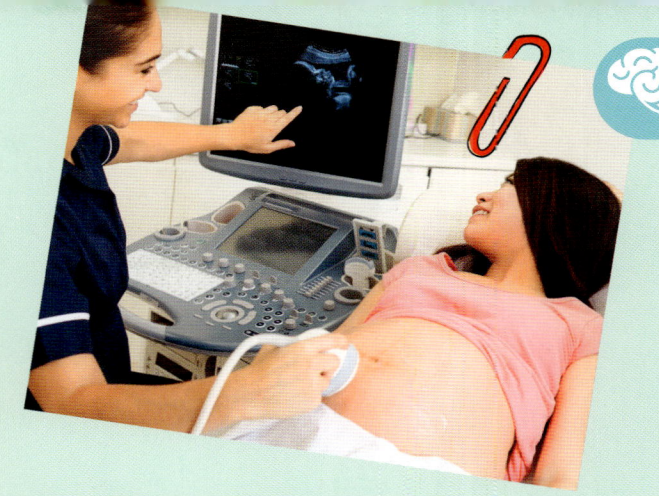

Hello, baby!

Ultrasounds are scans that show how the baby is developing inside the womb. **Sound waves** produced by the scanner are used to create a clear picture on screen.

Feeding the baby

Babies can't eat solid food immediately after being born. They will need to drink milk that's either milk from human breasts, or a specially made formula.

Jumbo pregnancy

Some small mammals, such as hamsters, have pregnancy periods that last only 2-3 weeks. Elephants set the record for the longest pregnancy period of any mammal, with pregnancies lasting 22 months - almost two years!

Breast milk and formula provide all the nutrients a baby needs.

Twins

Sometimes a person has **two babies** at the **same time**. They can look identical or completely different! They are known as twins.

Peas in a pod

Identical twins share the **same genes**, and are always the same sex: either two girls or two boys. Non-identical twins share half their genes, like all siblings.

Sixth sense

Some people believe that twins share a special sense. Sometimes one twin may seem to understand what the other is thinking without saying a word, or realize something is wrong without the other twin telling them.

The chance of having identical twins is about one in every 250 pregnancies.

Making a difference

Even identical twins have slightly different DNA. Our **experiences** and our **environment** can also change how our genes work. So twins and non-twins alike can all end up different from their family because of their own unique lives.

I prefer riding my scooter.

Big happy family

When multiple babies are born at once, they have different names.
- two babies – **twins**
- three babies – **triplets**
- four babies – **quadruplets**
- five babies – **quintuplets**
- six babies – **sextuplets**
- seven babies – **septuplets**
- eight babies – **octuplets**

I prefer reading.

Twin time

A history of twins in a family means it's more likely for **future generations** to have twins, too. Some medical treatments that help people have babies can also cause multiple births.

Skin deep

The skin is simply super! It is **waterproof**, strong, **protects** structures underneath it, and helps to **control** body temperature. Skin is also full of sensors that help us experience the environment.

Biggest organ
Skin is the largest organ in the human body. It forms about 15 per cent of body weight.

Skin flakes
The body sheds about 2 million dead skin cells every hour. Dust is partially made up of these dead skin flakes. New skin cells are produced all the time, so our skin is renewed every month.

Skin layers
The top layer of skin is the epidermis, which is partly made of dead or dying cells that you can see. Below that is the dermis, which is full of sweat glands, blood vessels, nerves, and hair roots.

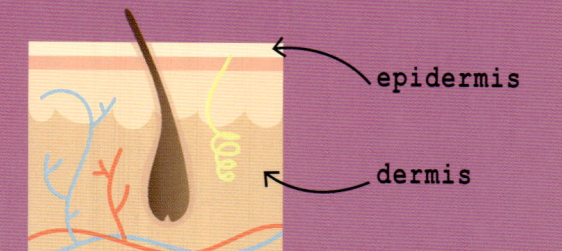

epidermis
dermis

Wrapping paper
Everything in the body is wrapped up by skin. It's the perfect wrapping paper. It stops germs getting into the body. Water bounces off the skin's surface, as it is waterproof. Skin also keeps water in, so the body doesn't dry out.

Moles and more

Some people have natural markings on the skin, such as freckles, moles, and birthmarks. Freckles can also be caused by sunlight. These small dots appear in groups, usually on the nose and cheeks, because the sun's UV rays trigger cells in the skin to overproduce colour pigment. Skin markings are almost always harmless, but check with a doctor if you notice a mole or freckle change shape or colour.

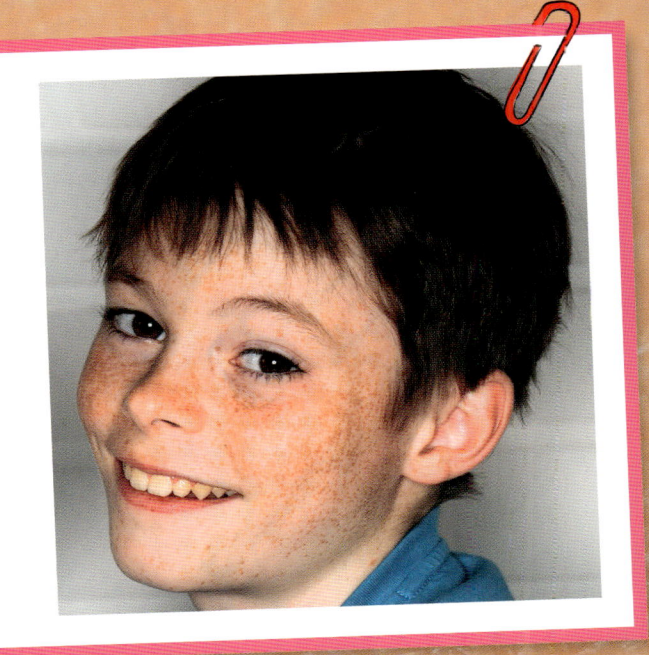

Thick and thin

Skin on the eyelids is very thin. That's why blood vessels can sometimes be seen underneath this thin skin. The soles of the feet have thick skin to cope with the body's weight and contact with the rough ground.

Melanin

Skin colour depends on how much pigment – or melanin – there is. Dark skin contains more melanin than light skin. Freckles are patches where there is a lot of melanin. Some people have albinism, which means they have little or no melanin. This gives them very pale skin and hair, and can affect their eye colour and eyesight.

Temperature control

When body temperature goes up, sweat glands start working to produce sweat. Sweat helps cool the body down. When the body feels cold, hairs on the skin stand up, which helps to trap in heat to keep us warm.

Body temperature

Body temperature is always about 37 degrees Celsius (98.6 degrees Fahrenheit). This temperature lets the body **carry out its functions**.

Temperature control

Temperature **sensors** exist all over the body. They send **messages** to the brain to tell it if the body is too **hot** or **cold**. The body then decides whether it needs to warm up or cool down. This system is called thermoregulation.

Thermogram

Pictures called thermograms show body temperature. Body parts close to the **heart** are **warm** and show up as red. **Cooler** body parts, such as **fingers** and **toes**, show up as purple or blue.

These thermograms show a body that is cold, a body that is normal temperature, and one that is very hot.

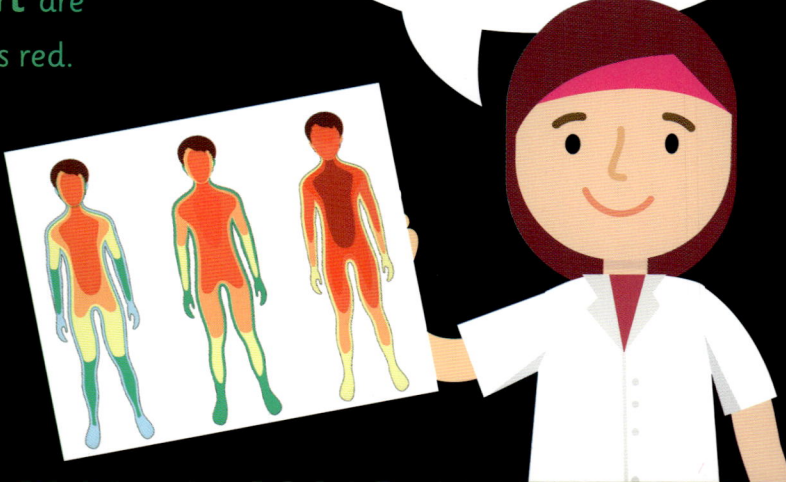

Keep it steady

We can help our bodies keep an **ideal temperature** by wearing the right clothes for the weather. People with certain medical conditions take particular care to help regulate their body temperatures, as some symptoms can get worse when it's too hot or too cold.

Too hot

To cool down, **blood vessels** in the skin **become wider** to let heat out of the blood. Sweating also cools us.

Too cold

To warm up, **blood vessels** in the skin **become thinner** to reduce heat loss. The body may shiver, generating heat.

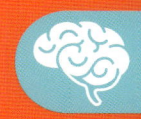

Warm-blooded

Mammals and birds are warm-blooded creatures. This means they **maintain their body temperature** by making their own body heat.

Even if it's freezing outside, polar bears can keep their bodies toasty warm.

Cold-blooded

Reptiles and lizards are cold-blooded, so they **cannot make their own body heat**. Their body temperature isn't constant, as they take on the temperature around them.

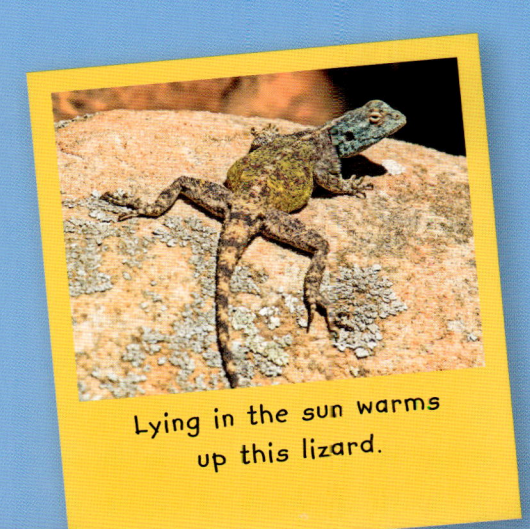

Lying in the sun warms up this lizard.

Hairy story

Hair isn't just for decoration — it helps **protect parts of the body**. That's why hair grows on your head, arms, legs, and face.

Curly hair

Straight or curly?
Follicles in the skin come in different **shapes**. Straight-shaped follicles make **straight** hair. Follicles that are oval-shaped make **curly** hair.

Hair ABOVE the skin is dead. The living

Follicles
Hair begins below the surface of the skin. This hidden part is the **hair follicle**. Cells here increase in number, making hair grow longer.

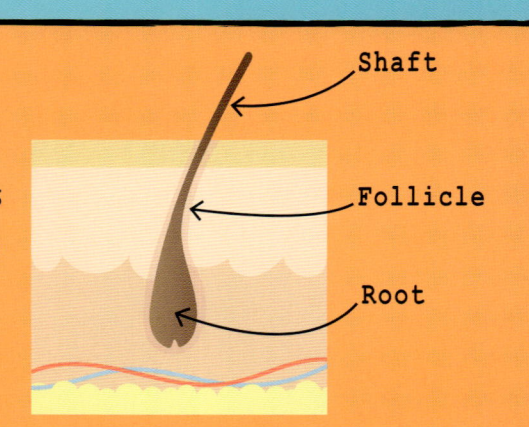

Shaft
Follicle
Root

86

Straight hair

Hair types

"Vellus" hair is **soft**, **fine hair** found across the face, abdomen, arms, and legs. "Terminal" hair is **thick hair** on the head. It grows on the face and in the armpits when people reach adolescence.

Vellus hair

Terminal hair

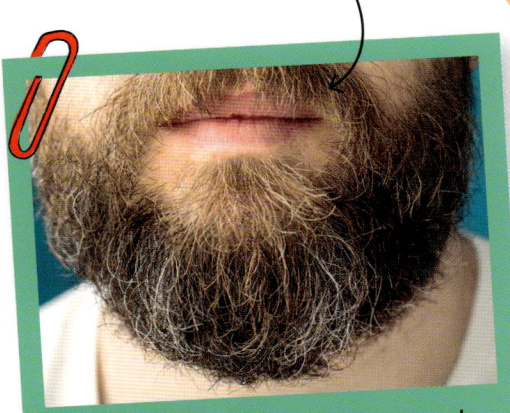

Terminal hair is tougher and gives more protection to soft places on the body.

part of hair LIES BENEATH the skin.

Genetics

Hair colour is determined by the **genes** inherited from your genetic family. Red hair is the **rarest** colour. Only **2 per cent** of people in the world have red hair.

Temperature control

Hair keeps the **head warm** during winter. It does this by **trapping warm air**. It also helps to protect the scalp from **sunburn** in the heat.

87

Brain box

How **brilliant** is the brain? It is the **control centre**, giving **instructions** to the whole body. Most of this happens without you **realizing** it.

Left and right
The brain has **two sides**. People used to think the left side was the **analytical** half, and the right side the **creative** half. But the brain is complex and most of the time the two halves work together.

Headache pain feels like it's in the brain, but it's not. The pain is picked up by sensors in the layers around the brain.

No pain
The brain **can't feel pain** as it doesn't have any pain receptors. That means brain surgery can be carried out on patients who are awake!

Rewiring

The brain **rewires** itself through life. If we learn a new word, then **new connections** are formed in the brain that help us remember the word. If we have an injury and we forget some words, our brains can find a **new way** for us to learn and remember them.

Dyslexia can cause issues with reading, writing, and spelling. But it also has some advantages, like good puzzle-solving skills.

Your brain works differently to everyone else's. That means everyone interacts with the world uniquely.

The brain is constantly learning. Mistakes help it learn quickly and get better at solving problems.

Lost in thought

Are you a daydreamer? Or are you too focused to get distracted? Or are you both? Sometimes it's fun to see where your **imagination takes you**!

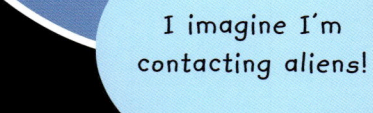

I imagine I'm contacting aliens!

Always thinking
The brain is always **hard at work**. So even while the brain is **busy** controlling your movements, it can also be **forming thoughts**.

Imagine that
At the front of the brain is the **prefrontal cortex**, which is responsible for imagination. Other parts of the brain **supply it with information** to come up with new ideas.

Each person has natural reactions to situations. They make people feel a range of emotions. These feelings can be so powerful that you get a physical feeling in the head or tummy. They may make it hard to focus on other thoughts.

I'm so surprised I can't think what to say!

Memory lane

The brain **stores experiences** as memories. Talking about important memories and looking at photographs reinforces the memory. If the memories are less important, you can **forget them**.

The brain can store one petabyte of data, which is enough to store five billion books!

I imagine I'm jetting off to the moon!

Lifelong learning

Studying a subject at school, watching someone else, **listening to others**, and sharing feelings all help people to learn.

Look to the future

From a space shuttle to this book you're reading now, everything humans make comes from **our imagination**. Imagination helps people to change things, otherwise everything would stay the same all the time. What kind of future can you imagine?

Communication

Some people might think that **speaking** is the only way to **communicate**. But thanks to our bodies, there are lots of ways to express ourselves **without saying a word**!

Shaking the head = "no"

Nodding the head = "yes"

Gestures
Gestures (movements) can be used to communicate. Most people do it so often, they may not even notice. For example, we use gestures to say "hello", "stop", and "good job." Gestures may mean different things in different countries.

"Please" in American Sign Language

"Please" in British Sign Language

Sign language
This group of silent facial expressions and hand gestures can be used in place of spoken language. The hands are so flexible that they can create gestures to represent all the words. Different countries use different sign languages.

Spoken language

The voice is produced from the vocal cords, which are two tissue flaps inside the throat. Air makes them vibrate, making sound.

The tongue and lips convert the vibration sound from the throat into speech that comes out of the mouth.

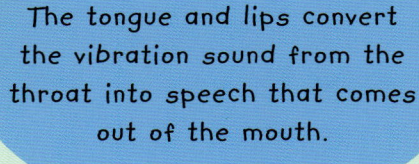

Facial expressions

Faces can communicate feelings by their different expressions. A smile that wrinkles around the eyes shows genuine happiness, while a furrowed forehead and downturned mouth show the exact opposite!

Smelling

Animals make noises and body gestures just like people, but their communication isn't as advanced as human languages. But, unlike humans, some animals also use their own scent to leave signals for other animals to communicate with them.

Body language

Open body language – open arms, upturned palms, and relaxed legs – usually indicates feeling friendly, calm, and approachable. Closed body language – folded arms, clenched hands, and crossed legs – suggests the person is feeling angry, worried, or vulnerable.

93

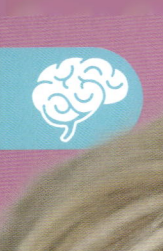

Face to face

The face gives you character and shows how **you're feeling**. But are you **in control** of the movements the face makes?

Flexible face
Facial expressions are produced by **muscles** that **pull in different directions**. Facial muscles join to the skin instead of bones. This means even the tiniest movement can show up on the face.

About 50 different facial muscles combine to create every facial expression.

Blinks and winks
Sometimes the muscles move automatically, like **when you blink**. Muscles can also be moved deliberately. **Winking takes an active effort**, unlike blinking.

Look closely! Sometimes our face shows how we are truly feeling automatically, like a sad frown. Other times it is possible to hide your true feelings with active effort, like forcing a smile.

Happiness

Lips lifted and rosy cheeks

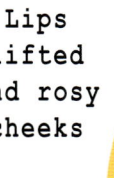

Anger

Eyebrows frowning and tight lips

One in five people can use FACIAL MUSCLES to wiggle their ears.

Express yourself

The human face can make a wide range of facial expressions. This makes our faces a great way to **communicate without words**. Let's look at some different expressions.

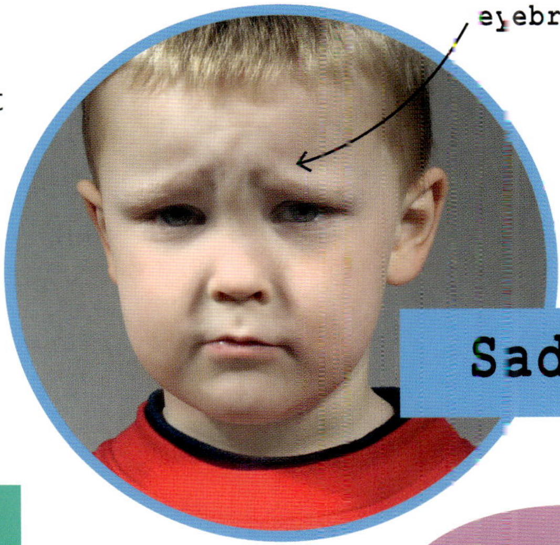

Sadness

Lips turned down and inner corners of eyebrows raised

Surprise

Mouth open and eyebrows lifted

Hard to read

Not everyone can **read expressions** or work out how others are feeling. Some find it hard to show how they are feeling with expressions. If you're unsure how someone is feeling by looking at their face, you can ask them.

How are you feeling?

95

Pearly whites

Tough teeth have a **hard outer** shell to protect the **soft inside**. After you lose your baby teeth, the second set are the only ones you'll ever get, so keeping teeth **clean and shiny** is essential.

During the average lifetime, a total of 80 days are spent brushing the teeth!

A garden snail has 14,000 tiny little teeth!

By the age of six, you have 52 teeth, but most of those are big teeth still waiting to come out.

Milk teeth
Babies get **20 small teeth** known as "milk teeth". They are **softer** and have **less protection** than adult teeth, so taking care of them is important.

Permanent teeth
Milk teeth start **falling out** by the age of around six. They are replaced by **32 bigger teeth**, which are permanent and can't naturally regrow.

Inside a tooth

The white part of the tooth is the **crown**. It is made of hard enamel. **Roots** hold the tooth in place.

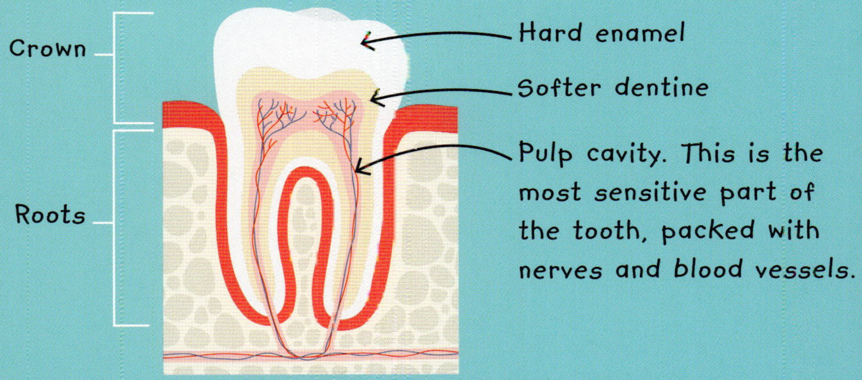

- Crown
- Roots
- Hard enamel
- Softer dentine
- Pulp cavity. This is the most sensitive part of the tooth, packed with nerves and blood vessels.

Teeth can sometimes erupt at odd angles, which can make it hard for a person to chew and bite. Braces can be used to train the teeth to grow back the right way.

Keeping clean

Brushing your teeth gets **rid of plaque** — a dirty layer of bacteria that builds up on teeth. Plaque can lead to bad breath and tooth decay.

Brush your teeth for at least two minutes, twice a day.

The main job of teeth is to start the digestion process by chewing and chomping through food in the mouth. Teeth break down food into pieces that can be swallowed, ready for the tummy.

Lots of liquids

The body oozes different fluids for different reasons — tiny holes in the skin **release sweat**, irritated eyes produce **tears**, and slimy **saliva** swims in the mouth.

Break into a sweat

Heat can activate **sweat glands** under the skin. When they are activated, sweat droplets rise to the surface and out through tiny holes in the skin called **pores**. This helps to cool the body down.

The body produces at least 3 litres (6 pints) of sweat every day.

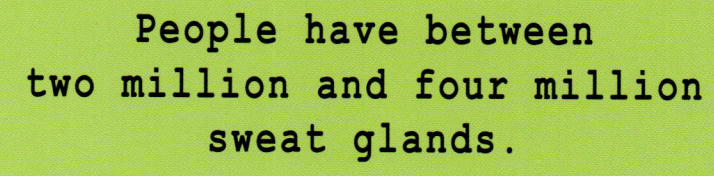

People have between two million and four million sweat glands.

Slimy saliva

Salivary glands produce saliva throughout the day, keeping the **mouth moist**. This makes **speaking** and **eating easier**. Natural chemicals in saliva help kill harmful germs in the mouth.

99 per cent of saliva is water.

TEARS taste salty because they contain NATURAL SALTS.

Dry your eyes

Above the eyes are **tear glands**. Tears from these glands drain down tubes called **tear ducts** in the nose. But when there are too many tears, they spill out in the form of crying.

Tears can form for a few reasons:

- Tears clean and **moisten** the eyes to keep them healthy.
- Tears **wash away** anything that is **irritating the eyes**, such as dust or pollen.
- **Emotional tears** can form when someone has strong feelings.

Oxygen's journey

When we breathe in we **take in** oxygen, one of the invisible gases in air. Cells use oxygen like fuel, **powering them up** to keep the body going.

Carbon dioxide

oxygen

Nasal cavity
Oral cavity
Larynx
Trachea
Bronchi
Bronchioles
Right lung
Left lung
Diaphragm

Trees and plants produce oxygen that we need and take in carbon dioxide that we don't need.

Waste products

Cells that run on oxygen produce a gas called **carbon dioxide** as they work hard. This gas is not wanted in the body, so the respiratory system works to **take it away**.

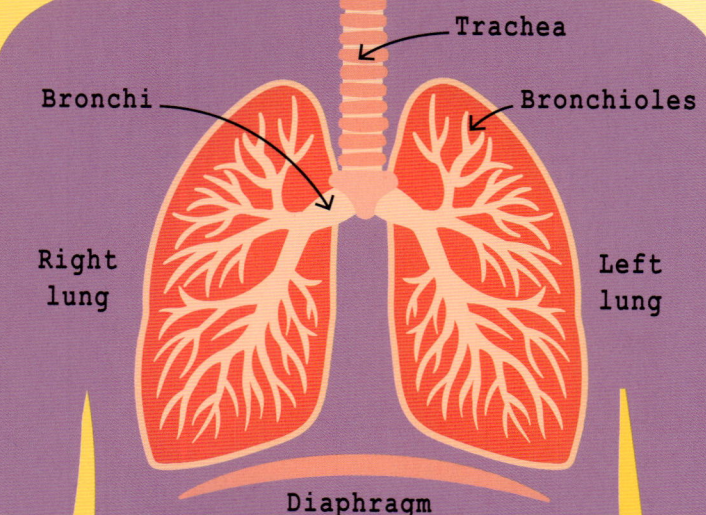

Muscle movement

Without the diaphragm muscle, breathing couldn't happen. It moves **down** when breathing in, helping the lungs **expand**. When it **relaxes upwards**, it moves air back out of the lungs. Other muscles, such as those between the ribs, help to expand the ribcage when a person breathes.

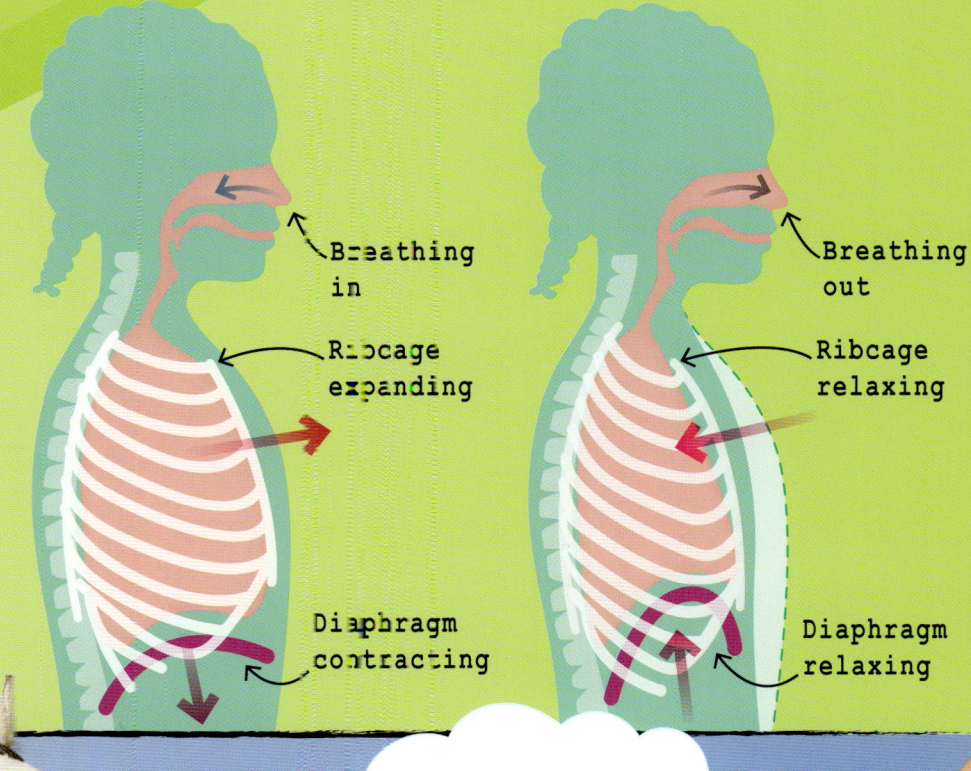

Hiccups occur when the diaphragm spasms, making you take a quick breath that hits your vocal cords.

- Breathing in
- Ribcage expanding
- Diaphragm contracting
- Breathing out
- Ribcage relaxing
- Diaphragm relaxing

A human can breathe through their nose and mouth. A horse can only breathe through its nose.

Asthma

Some people have a condition called asthma, which can sometimes make breathing difficult. It often happens **after exercise** or **in cold weather**. People with asthma can use a little tool called an **inhaler** to help ease or prevent their symptoms.

Asthma inhaler

Take a breath

Breathing in and out is **vital** for staying **alive**. So what body parts are involved in this important job?

Children aged 6-9 breathe in and out between 12 and 16 times every minute.

How air travels

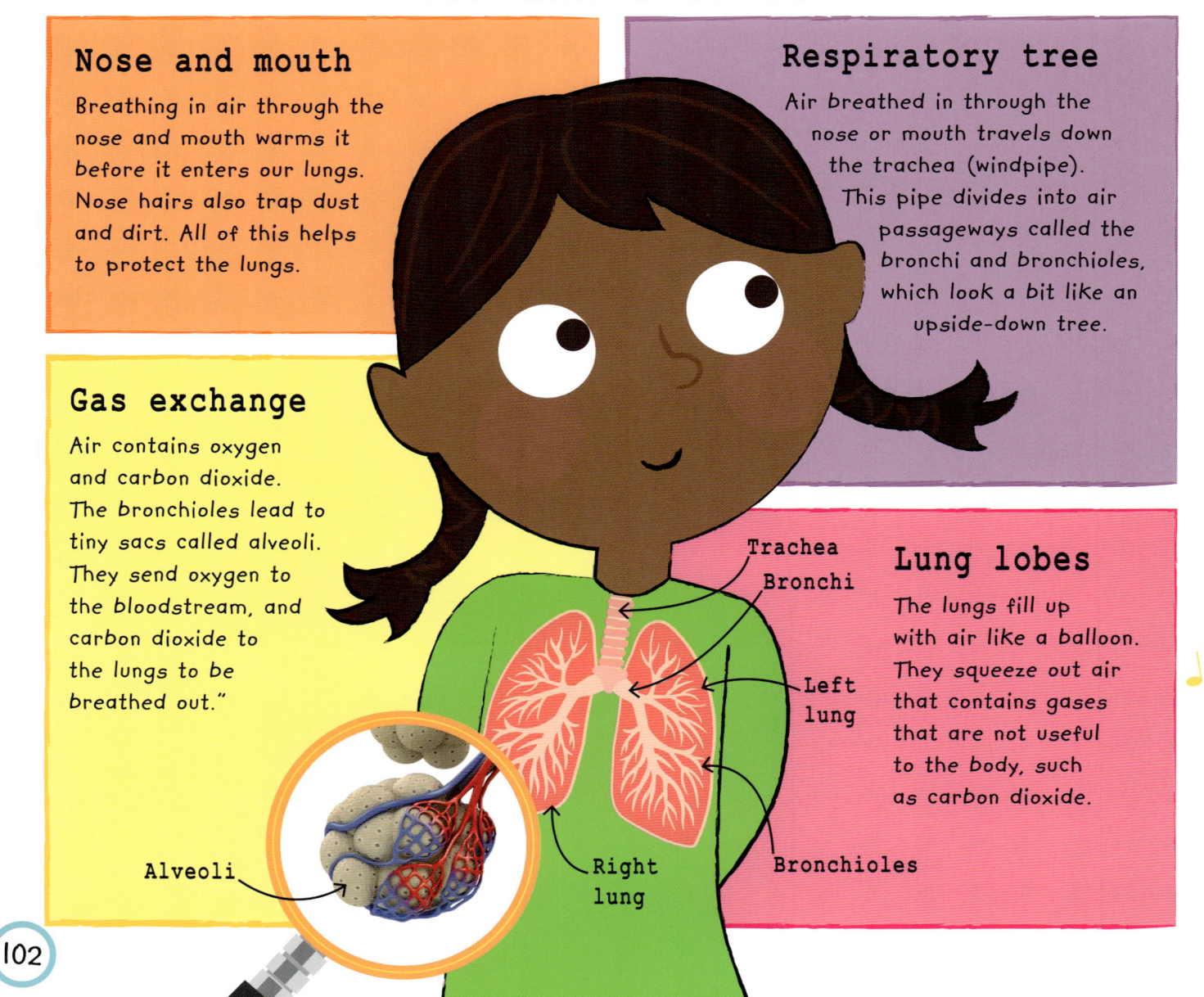

Nose and mouth
Breathing in air through the nose and mouth warms it before it enters our lungs. Nose hairs also trap dust and dirt. All of this helps to protect the lungs.

Respiratory tree
Air breathed in through the nose or mouth travels down the trachea (windpipe). This pipe divides into air passageways called the bronchi and bronchioles, which look a bit like an upside-down tree.

Gas exchange
Air contains oxygen and carbon dioxide. The bronchioles lead to tiny sacs called alveoli. They send oxygen to the bloodstream, and carbon dioxide to the lungs to be breathed out."

Lung lobes
The lungs fill up with air like a balloon. They squeeze out air that contains gases that are not useful to the body, such as carbon dioxide.

Trachea
Bronchi
Left lung
Right lung
Bronchioles
Alveoli

102

Noisy breathing

Breathing can be **noisy** when a part of the breathing tract is narrowed. Snoring occurs when the nose or throat is **blocked**.

Free divers

People who dive deep into the ocean without any breathing equipment are called free divers. They train so that they can **hold their breath** for a long time underwater.

Singing

Belting out tunes is really good for you! Singing **uses all the muscles** used in breathing and helps to make them stronger.

Lungs could float on water since they are filled with air.

Heart of the matter

Your **heart pumps** away every second. It is the centre of the cardiovascular system, which **sends blood** around the body.

Right atrium

All heart
The heart is a **muscular organ** that pumps blood around the body. Blood contains the **oxygen** and **nutrients** that the body's organs and tissues need to work properly.

Change of heart
You may feel your heart speed up when you are **excited** or **scared**. This allows more **oxygen to rush to your brain and muscles** in preparation for action.

Artery carrying oxygen-rich blood from the heart to the arm

Side to side
The right side of the heart sends blood that is low in oxygen (**oxygen-poor**) to the lungs to collect more oxygen. The left side of the heart sends the blood that has lots of oxygen in it (**oxygen-rich**) around the body.

Left atrium

Vein carrying oxygen-poor blood from the body back to the heart

Left ventricle

Secret chambers
The heart has **four chambers: two atria and two ventricles**. Every chamber has a one-way valve to make sure blood only flows forwards, not backwards.

Right ventricle

Heartbeat helper
A **pacemaker** is a device that is surgically fitted under the skin to **correct irregular heartbeats**. It produces electrical signals to keep the heart beating at a healthy rate, and lasts about five years.

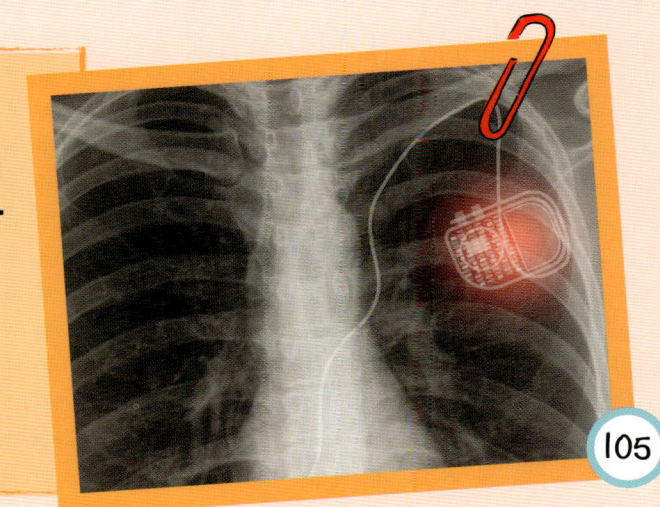

A rush of blood

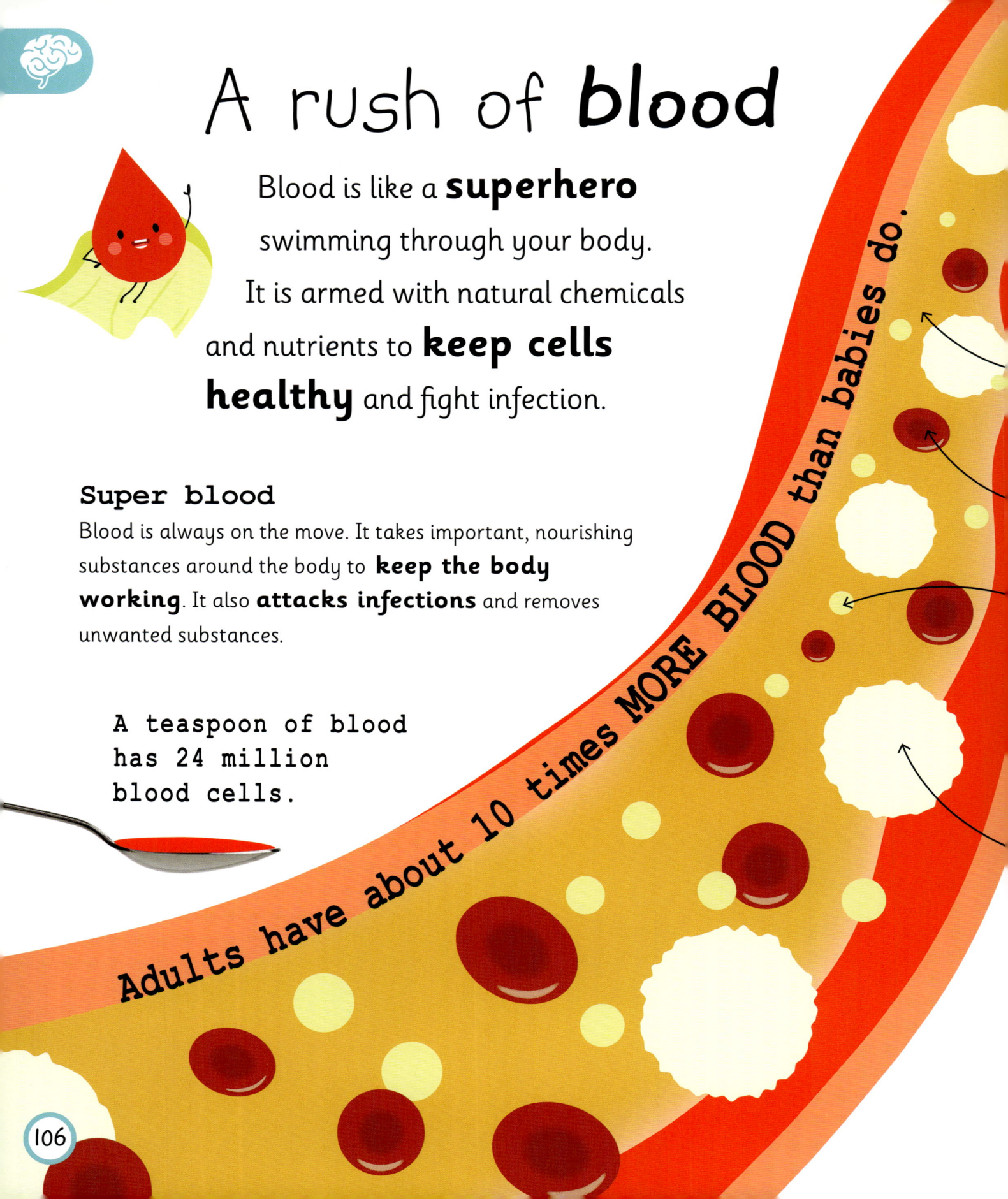

Blood is like a **superhero** swimming through your body. It is armed with natural chemicals and nutrients to **keep cells healthy** and fight infection.

Super blood

Blood is always on the move. It takes important, nourishing substances around the body to **keep the body working**. It also **attacks infections** and removes unwanted substances.

A teaspoon of blood has 24 million blood cells.

Adults have about 10 times MORE BLOOD than babies do.

All human blood is red, even though veins look blue. However, octopuses really do have blue blood.

What's in blood?

Plasma
More than half of blood is a **watery fluid** called plasma.

Red blood cells
Red blood cells carry oxygen around the body. There are more red blood cells than any other cells.

Platelets
If someone bleeds, platelets **help the blood to clot** and seal the wound.

White blood cells
White blood cells **attack any signs of infection** by surrounding them, or creating special proteins designed to destroy them.

Red blood cells are so tiny that 5,000 red blood cells could fit inside this full stop.

Donating blood
Blood donors are adults who **give some of their blood** to help people who need extra blood. A donor only donates a bit of blood, and then their **body will make more** to replace it.

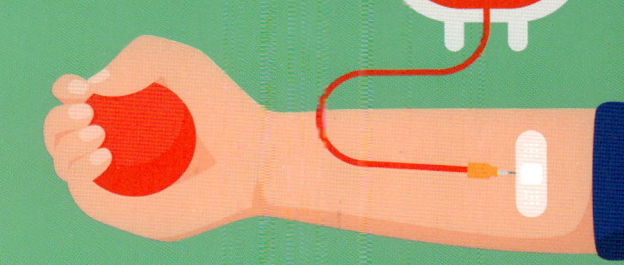

Blood transfusions
Patients who have **lost blood** and **need it replaced** can use blood donated by others. Giving a person **extra blood** is called a blood transfusion. Blood is grouped into different types. The new blood must match the patient's blood type.

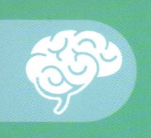

Circulation cycle

The circulatory system is made up of **blood vessels** (thin tubes), and the **blood** that travels within them.

The **heart** is central to the **circulatory system**. The right side of the heart sends blood to the lungs to collect **oxygen**, which the body needs to survive. The left side of the heart sends the oxygen-rich blood around the body.

— Arteries carrying oxygen-rich blood
— Veins carrying oxygen-poor blood

Heart

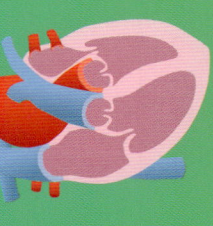

Lung vessels

Kidney vessels

Head vessels

Upper limb vessels

Liver vessels

Blood with lots of oxygen is bright red. Blood with low oxygen is dark red.

108

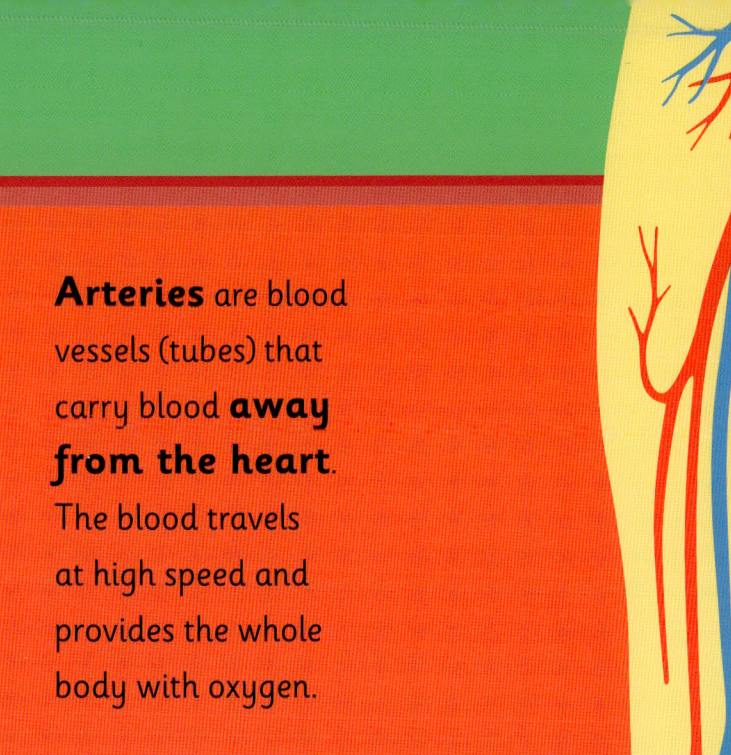

Blood travels all the way around the body up to three times every minute!

Lower limb vessels

Veins are blood vessels that carry blood **back to the heart**. They have **valves** like gates that only open in one direction. This helps blood travel back to the heart from the legs.

If all the blood vessels in an adult body were laid end to end, they would be able to go around the world 2.5 times!

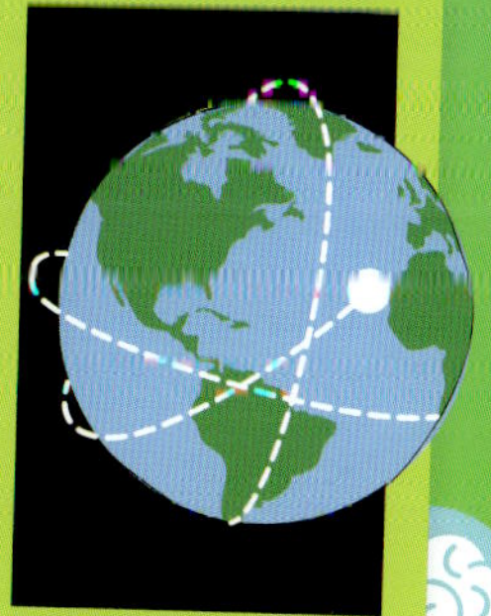

Capillaries

Arteries are blood vessels (tubes) that carry blood **away from the heart**. The blood travels at high speed and provides the whole body with oxygen.

If someone needs to have a body part amputated (removed), doctors change the blood vessels so the circulatory system still works.

109

Looking at lymph

The lymphatic system is part of the **body's defence**. It cleans up fluid, called lymph, which has leaked out of blood vessels. The system is made up of tubes, and groups of cells called lymph nodes.

Swollen foot

Lymph vessels

Lymph nodes

Liquid lymph
It's normal for lymph fluid to **leak** out of blood vessels, but it needs to go back into the bloodstream. If it doesn't, the body would **swell**.

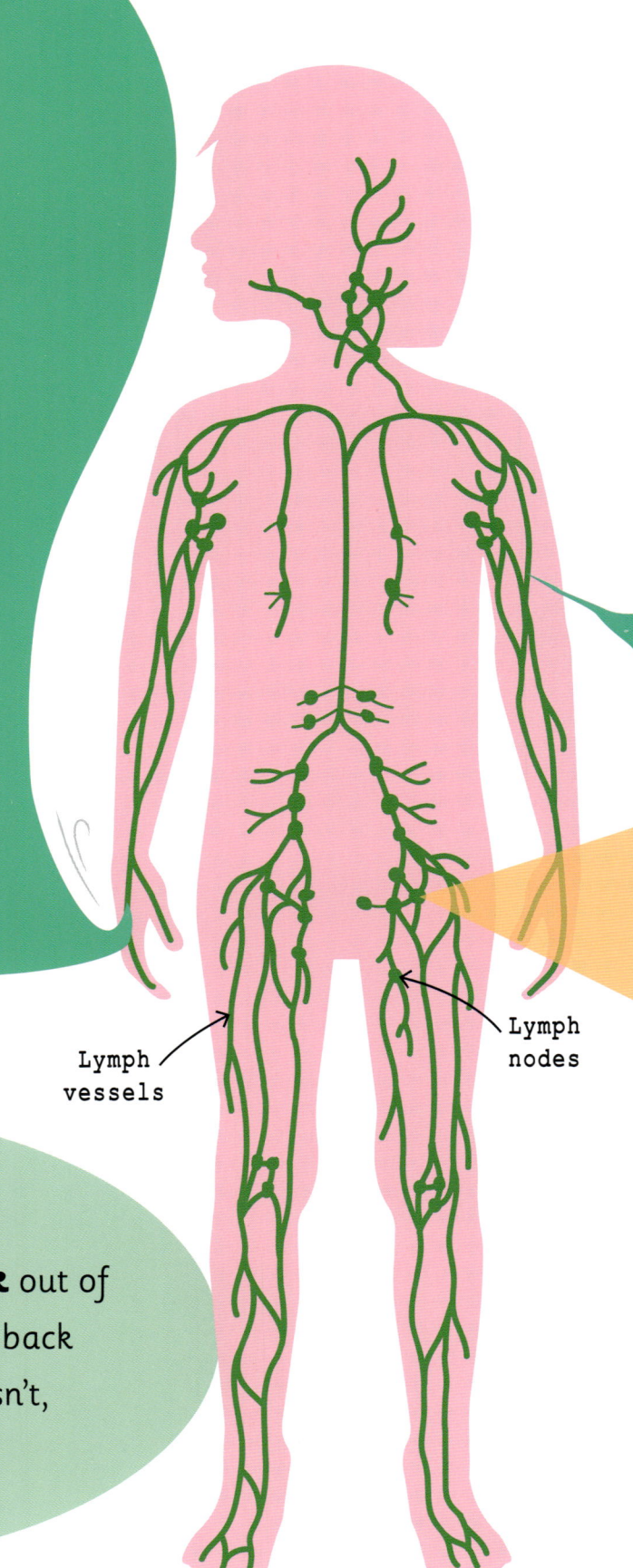

Tidying tools

Lymph vessels (thin tubes) **collect** up the lymph fluid to keep things clean and tidy.

The lymph vessels send the fluid into lymph nodes. These nodes contain cells that **fight infections** to help protect the body.

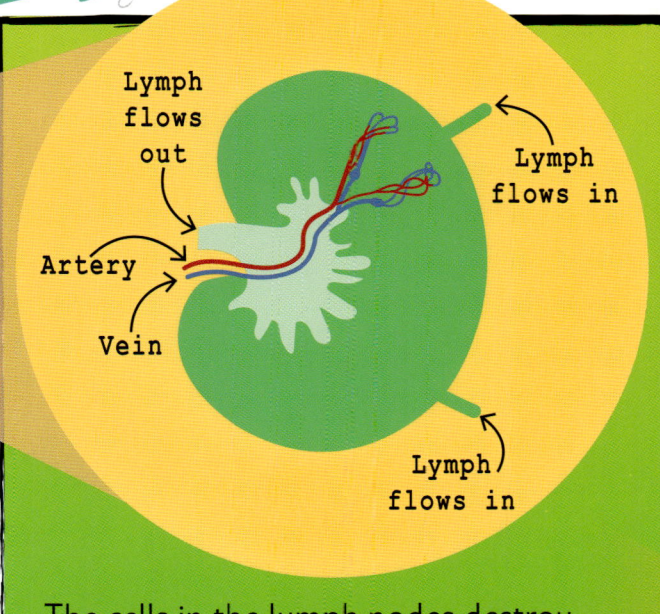

Lymph flows out
Lymph flows in
Artery
Vein
Lymph flows in

The cells in the lymph nodes destroy infections that they find in the lymph fluid. Then the cleaned up lymph fluid is **returned to the bloodstream**.

Lymph can only travel in one direction. The many valves in lymph vessels keep the fluid moving one way.

There are loads of lymph nodes in your armpits!

Cleaning up

Every cell in the body produces **waste**. The body keeps the **blood healthy** by filtering out this waste. Organs including the **liver** and **kidneys** are part of this clean-up crew.

If there is an issue with one kidney, it can be removed, and the body can live with just one.

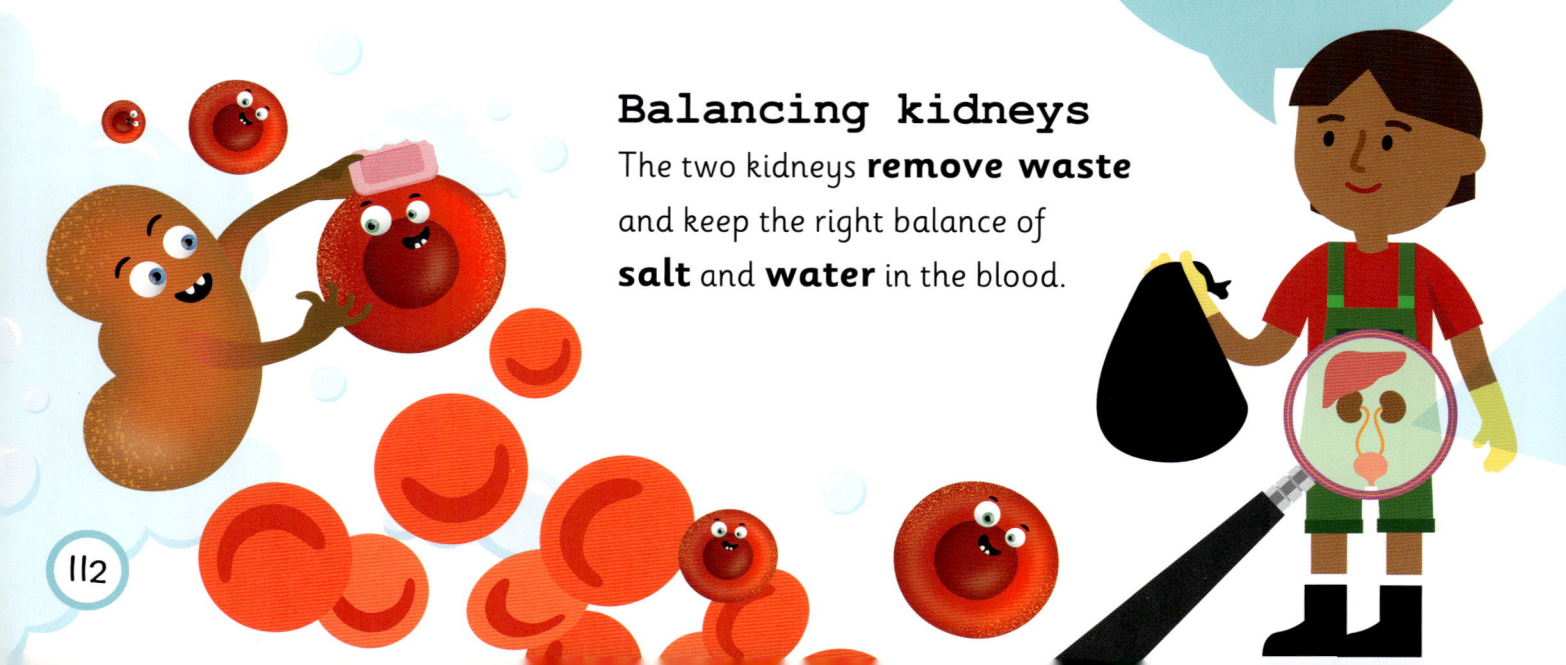

Balancing kidneys
The two kidneys **remove waste** and keep the right balance of **salt** and **water** in the blood.

Multitasking liver

The liver turns **nutrients** from food into energy, and removes **harmful substances** from blood. It also makes **bile**, a substance that breaks down fat.

Tube travel

Inside the kidneys, **waste** is turned into **urine** (wee). This travels through tubes called the ureters to the **bladder**. The bladder empties out wee through the **urethra**.

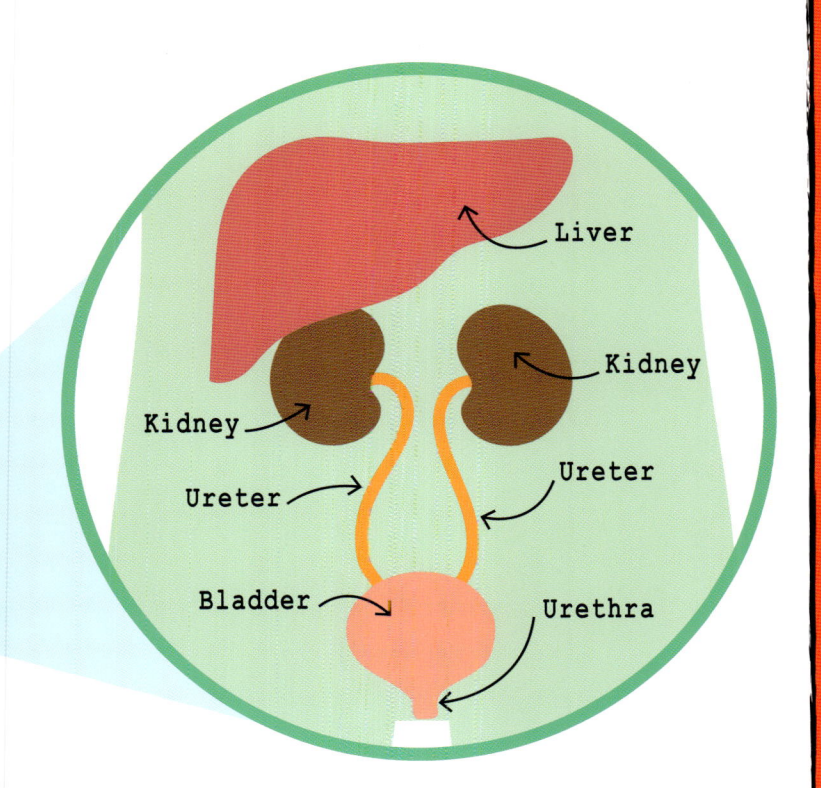

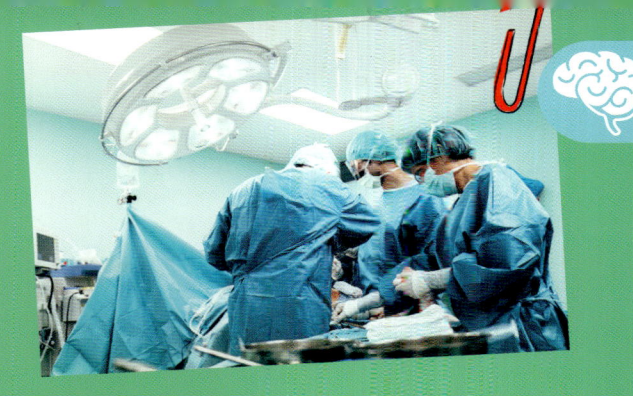

- Liver
- Kidney
- Kidney
- Ureter
- Ureter
- Bladder
- Urethra

Organ transplant

When the liver doesn't work well, it can sometimes be replaced. This is called a **liver transplant**. Surgeons can remove the **damaged** liver and put in a healthy one. A person can **donate** a part of their liver, and their own body will still work just fine.

Dialysis

The kidneys **clean blood**. If they can't do this, a **dialysis machine** can be used. This draws some blood out of the body, cleans it, and puts it back, without the patient feeling a thing.

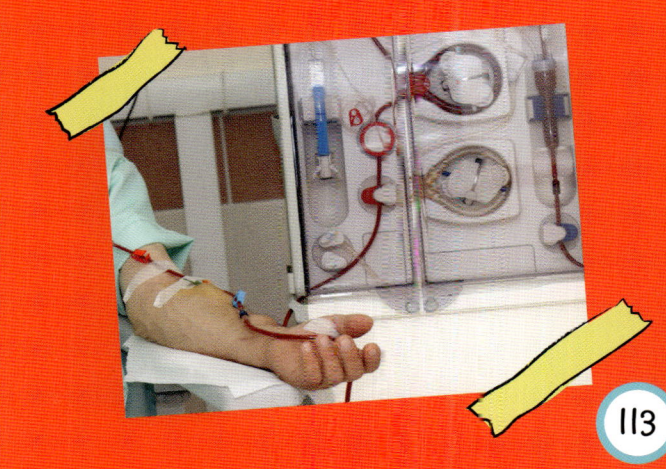

Eating adventure

Food goes on an incredible journey around the body. Its **nutrients** help to keep you strong, energized, and healthy, and the leftover **waste** ends up **down the toilet**!

Digestive delights

The digestive system manages the body's food intake. The role of this system is to **break down food** into basic nutrients that the body needs. These are **absorbed by the bloodstream** and taken to important body parts to keep everything **running smoothly**.

The average adult's digestive system measures 9 m (30 ft) – about the same length as two cars.

Some people cannot eat solid foods. Doctors may give them a tube leading directly into their stomach to give them the nutrients and energy they need.

A cow has a digestive system stretching 50 m (164 ft)!

Eventful journey

From the moment food enters the mouth, the **digestive process** gets underway. This is the very first stop on a long trip **around the body**, with plenty of stop-offs and a final exit!

Saliva forms in the mouth to make food moist and easier to swallow. Get ready to gulp!

Chewed food is swallowed down a long tube, called the oesophagus. It takes 10 seconds to travel from the throat to the stomach.

The stomach churns the food around for up to four hours until it becomes a creamy liquid known as chyme.

Chyme moves to the small intestine where important nutrients are absorbed into the blood. The bloodstream carries the nutrients all over the body wherever the cells need them.

The large intestine turns leftover chyme waste into poo that leaves via the bottom.

The average person spends about 100 DAYS of their life ON THE TOILET.

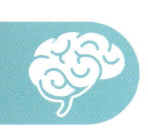

Little and large

The **intestines** have an important job in processing the food we eat. The small intestine absorbs **nutrients** (all the goodness in food). The large intestine absorbs **water** and produces **waste**.

Large intestine

Small intestine

Rectum

Small intestine
When food reaches the small intestine, it has already been **broken down** and mashed up by the stomach. It absorbs helpful **nutrients** from the food, and sends them to the **liver**.

Large intestine
The large intestine **reabsorbs** (takes in) water from the intestinal contents so that the body doesn't lose too much liquid. It also gets rid of **solid waste**.

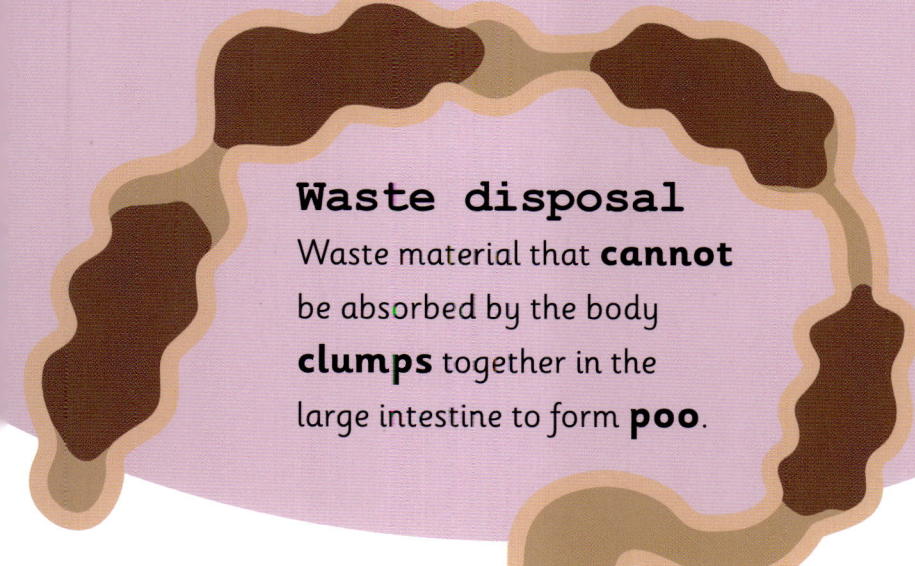

Waste disposal

Waste material that **cannot** be absorbed by the body **clumps** together in the large intestine to form **poo**.

End of the road

The **poo** stays in the **rectum** (the end of the large intestine). Nerves send messages to the brain to tell us to get rid of it. **Smelly gas** that formed in the intestines as food was broken down might also come out.

It takes 18-30 hours to process food and produce waste after eating.

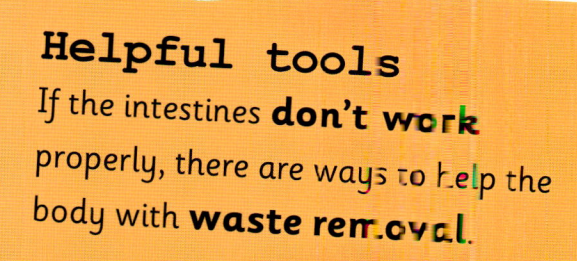

Helpful tools

If the intestines **don't work** properly, there are ways to help the body with **waste removal**.

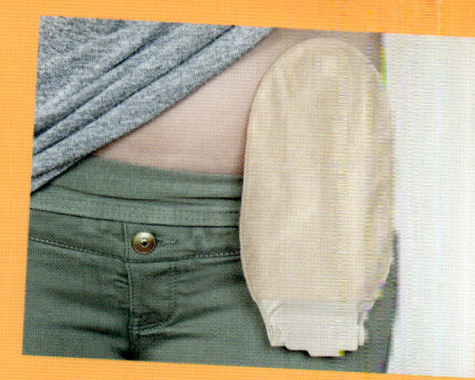

Some people need an operation to create a new opening in the body called a stoma. Waste comes out of the stoma and is stored in a pouch until the person removes and replaces it.

Drink up

There's a special part of the brain that detects when the body is **low on water**. It sends signals to the body to make us **drink fluids**.

Messengers
Hormones are chemical **messengers** sent from the brain to the body. They make you feel **thirsty** so you want to drink water. Drinking water increases a hormone that helps us feel satisfied.

Body signs
Changes in the body — such as **dry skin** or a **dry mouth** — can be signs that the body needs more water.

The urinary system

In an average lifetime, a person produces about 40,000 litres (85,000 pints) of wee. That's more than 200 full bath tubs!

Kidney — Kidney — Bladder

What is wee?

The urinary system produces wee (urine). The system helps keep the body's **fluid levels balanced**. If your wee is dark it usually means you're not drinking enough, and your body needs more liquid.

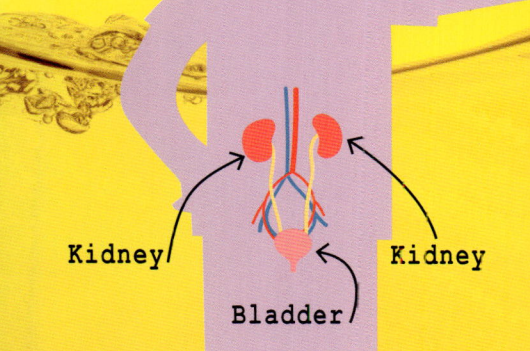

What's in wee?

About 95 per cent of wee is water. The rest is **waste products** from the body's cells and salts. Smelly wee could mean the body is dehydrated (it doesn't have enough water).

Wee was once used to make GUNPOWDER!

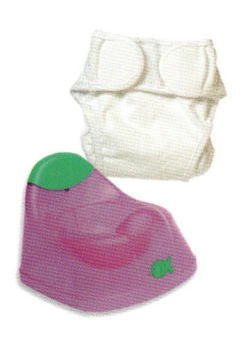

Bladder control

Wee is stored in the **bladder**. A very young child can't **control** their bladder well because their nervous system isn't developed enough. After it starts developing at age 2, children can learn to potty train.

Wee comes in different colours. It depends on what you eat and drink. Beetroot's pink colour also turns wee pink!

The need to wee

The **bladder's muscle stretches** when it is full of wee. This sends messages between the bladder and brain to say it's time to empty it out.

Coming to your senses

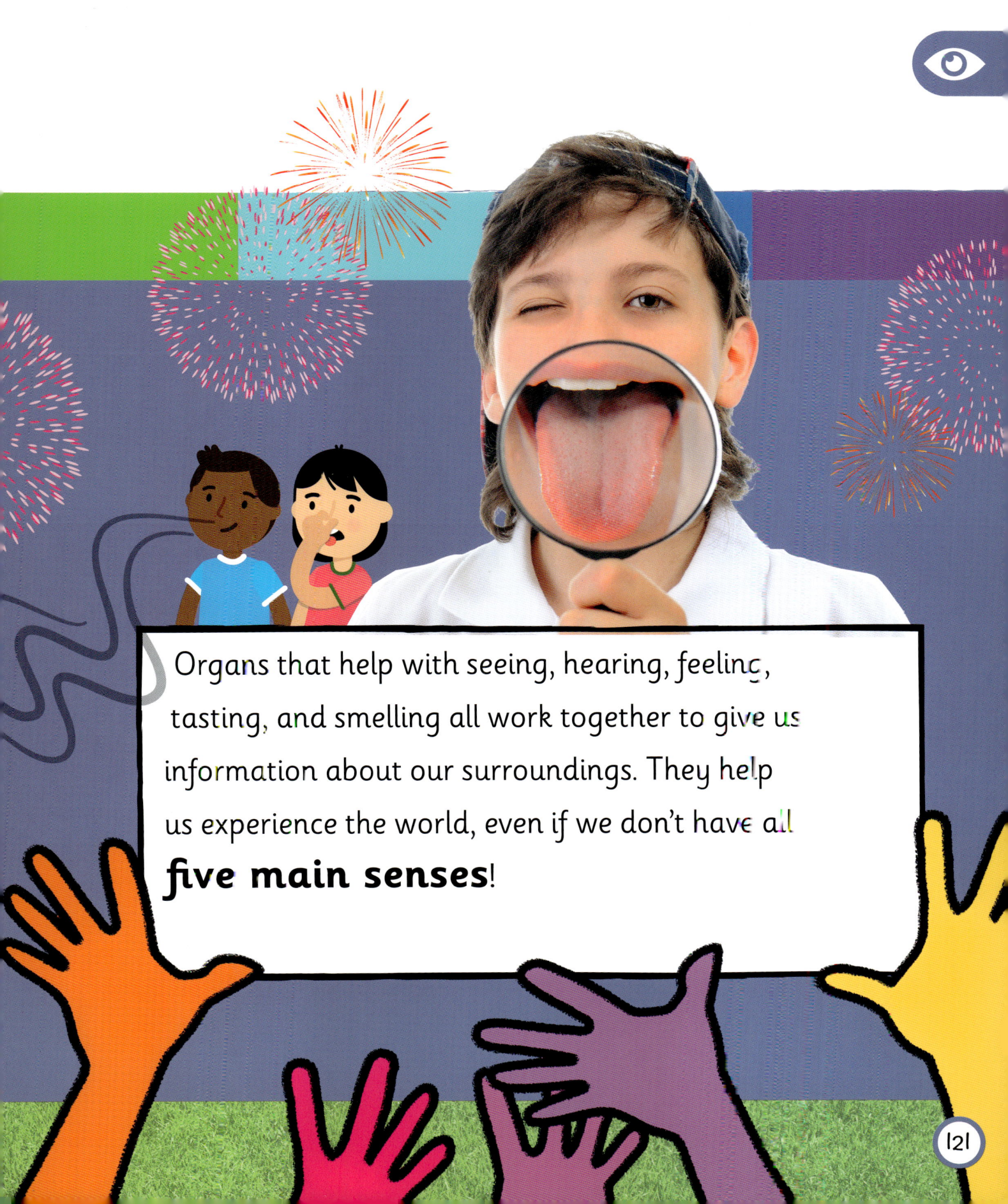

Organs that help with seeing, hearing, feeling, tasting, and smelling all work together to give us information about our surroundings. They help us experience the world, even if we don't have all **five main senses**!

Making sense

There are **five** main senses: **seeing**, **hearing**, **smelling**, **touching**, and **tasting**. They help us gather information about the world. Even if a person can't use all five senses, the **other senses** work together to help them figure out their surroundings.

Eyes for seeing
Each eyeball has **six muscles** that allow it to move in many directions. The optic nerve takes information from the eyes to the brain.

Ears for hearing
Ears **collect all sorts of sounds**. These travel through the different parts inside the ear to reach the brain, so it can make sense of all the noise.

Nose for smelling

Tiny smell particles, too small to see, bounce inside the nose. They **relay information to the brain**, telling it what smells good and what smells bad!

Hands for touching

The skin of the hands has thousands of **sense receptors**. These can sense different things, like whether something is hot or cold, soft or bumpy.

Tongue for tasting

The tongue is made of muscle that can **push food** around and break it into smaller pieces. It also has taste buds on it that sense different flavours.

Extra senses

There are other senses at work in the body, too. **Balance**, **hunger**, and certain instincts are other types of senses that a person can experience.

Eyes

There are **lots of layers** in each eye. Everything works together with the eye muscles, nerves, and the brain to **see** and **create pictures**.

Every iris is unique! No two people have the same iris. Even your left and right eyes are different.

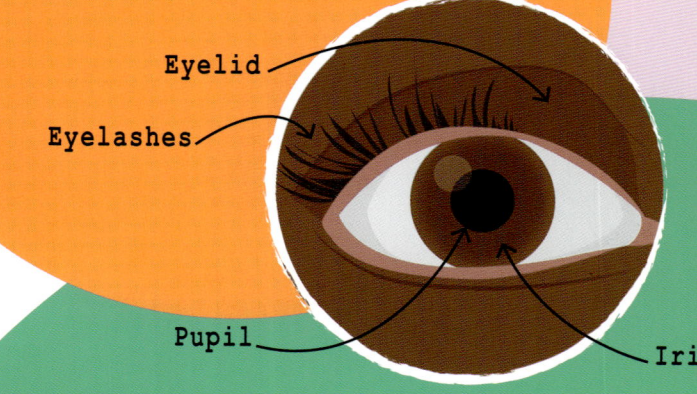

Eye protection
Eyelids help to **protect the eyes**, and eyelashes help to keep them **clean** by trapping dust and dirt.

Eyelid
Eyelashes
Pupil
Iris

Pupil and iris
The pupil is the **dark circle** in the eye. The iris, the **coloured** part, controls how much light gets in. When the iris gets bigger, the pupil gets smaller, and less light gets in.

Parts of the eye

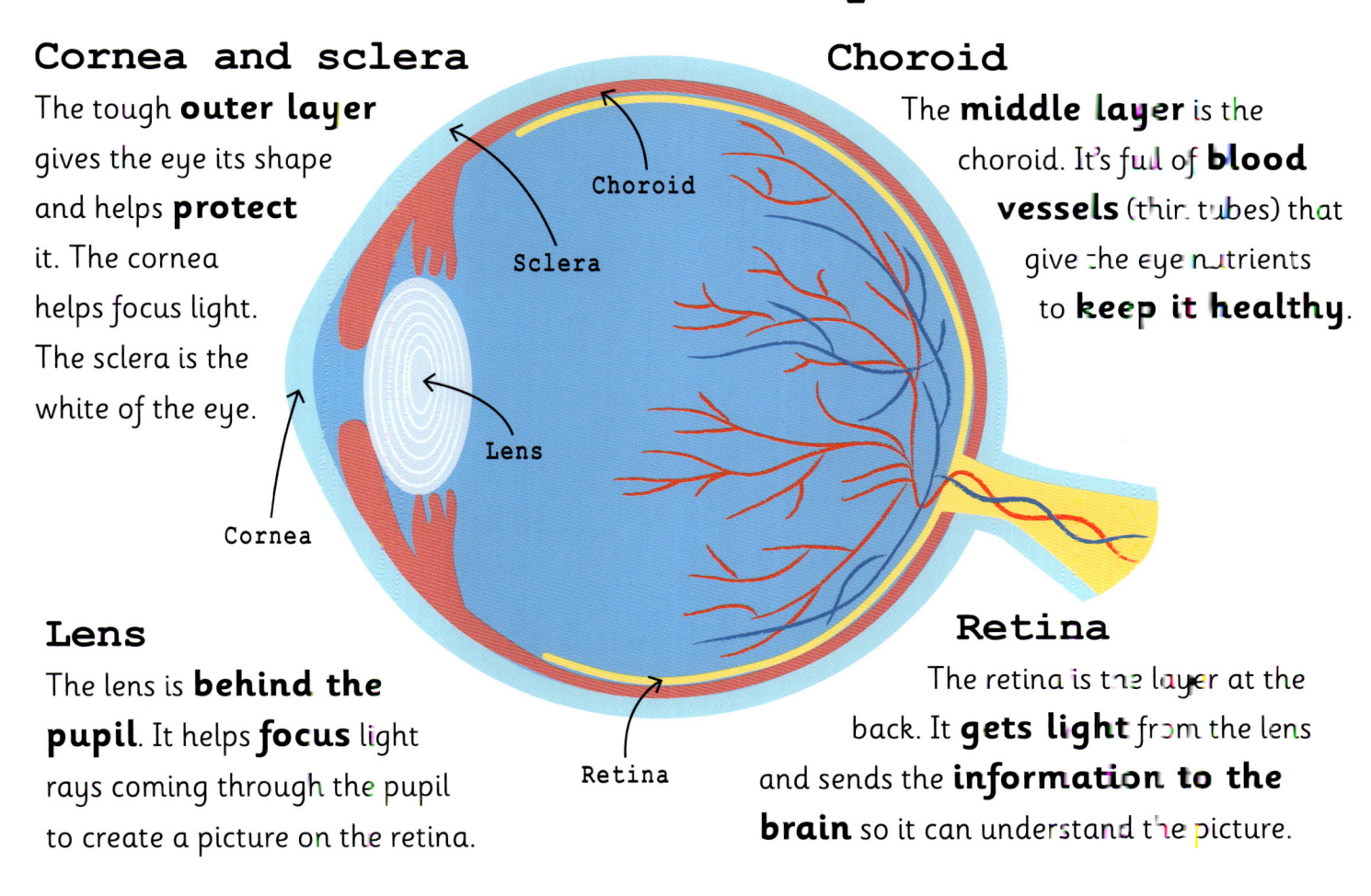

Cornea and sclera
The tough **outer layer** gives the eye its shape and helps **protect** it. The cornea helps focus light. The sclera is the white of the eye.

Choroid
The **middle layer** is the choroid. It's full of **blood vessels** (thin tubes) that give the eye nutrients to **keep it healthy**.

Lens
The lens is **behind the pupil**. It helps **focus** light rays coming through the pupil to create a picture on the retina.

Retina
The retina is the layer at the back. It **gets light** from the lens and sends the **information to the brain** so it can understand the picture.

Eyes can see up to 2 million colours!

Animal eyes
Prey animals are hunted by others, so they often have thin **horizontal** pupils. This means they can see across a wide space and spot enemy **predators**. **Vertical** pupils help predators see how far away their prey is.

Crocodile eye — Vertical pupil
Goat eye — Horizontal pupils
Frog eye

I have big eyes so that I can see animals that want to hurt me.

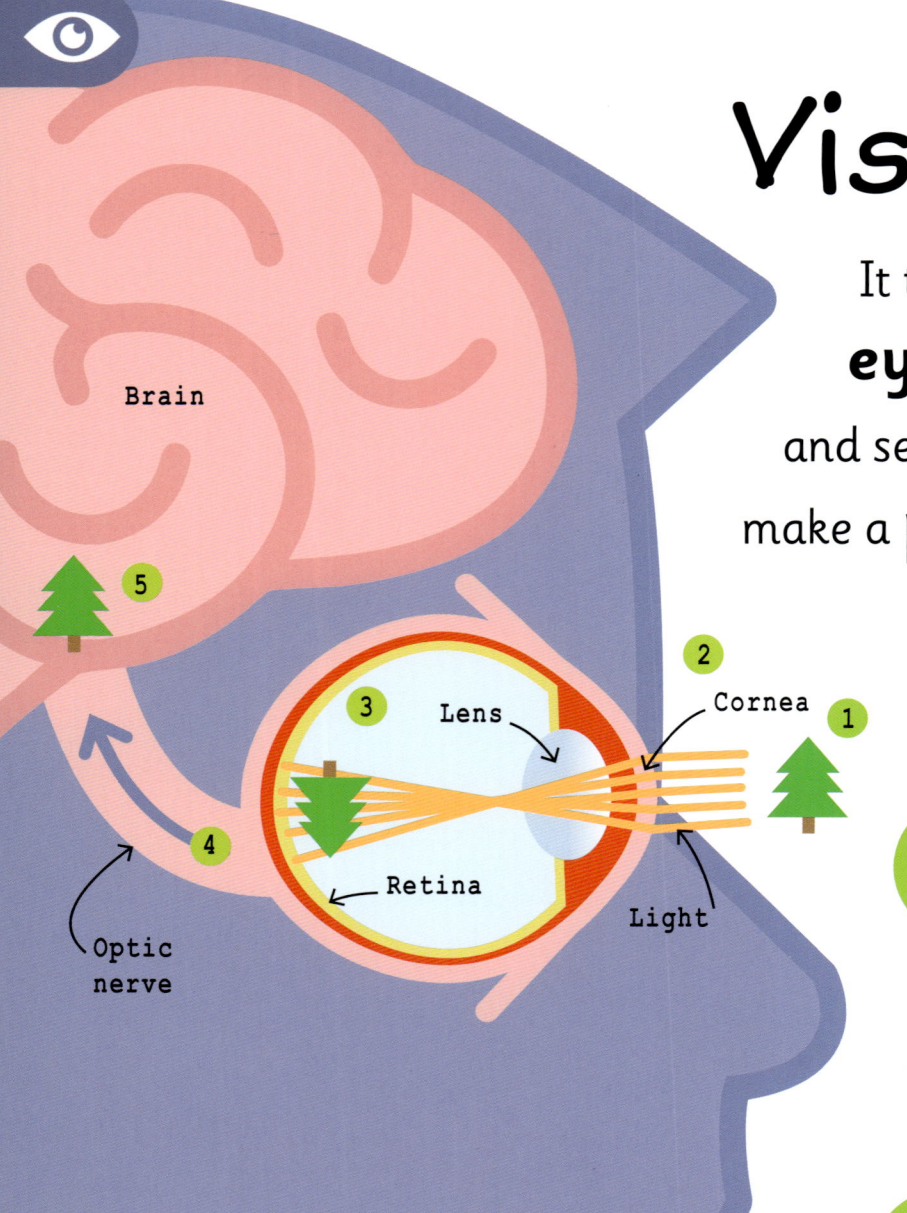

Vision

It takes many steps for the **eyes** to process information and send it to the **brain** to make a **picture**.

Brain

Lens
Cornea
Retina
Light
Optic nerve

How does vision work?

1 First, light bounces off of objects and into the eye.

2 The cornea and lens focus the light rays.

3 Light is processed by the retina in the back of the eye. But for now, the image is upside down!

4 The upside-down information travels to the brain along the optic nerve.

5 Finally, the brain puts together all the information and turns the image back the right way around again!

Hard to see

The eye has **lots of parts**, so if something doesn't work properly, it might mean a person can't see everything clearly. Eyesight often changes as people get older.

Glasses can have different types of lenses in them. The lenses focus light onto the retinas to help the eyes see clearly.

Some animals have great night vision, so it's easy for them to get around when it's dark.

Colour-blindness

Some people are colour-blind. This means they find it difficult to see the difference between certain colours.

Having trouble telling the difference between red and green is a common type of colour-blindness.

Try this colour vision test. Which circle has a 7, and which has a 13 in it?

Colour-blindness is more common in boys than in girls.

Optical illusions

Did you know your **eyes can play tricks** on you? They sometimes see things differently to what is really there, which can be **brain-boggling**!

In a muddle

The brain takes **information from the eyes** to work out what it is looking at. The brain usually gets it right, but it also uses **shortcuts** to process information quicker. If the brain becomes **confused**, it may see an optical illusion.

The eye usually takes a speedy 13 milliseconds to process an image!

On the move

Sometimes these swirls seem to be **moving**. The eyes see the repeated spiral pattern and the brain interprets the picture as moving. Staring at one spot helps **stop this effect**.

Shaping up

It seems there is a white **square** and **triangle** in these pictures, but the brain is being tricked! It assumes that the **blue shapes** are complete and are being **covered** by white shapes.

Just a mirage

Tired desert travellers may think they see a **pool of water** in the distance, but they never reach it. This is a mirage: a **layer of hot air** above the dunes that the brain mistakes for **water**.

The hole story

Pavement painters use shadows to make incredible pictures that look like they are **3-D** (three-dimensional).

Am I a duck or a rabbit?

Tricky

Artists can draw **a picture** that looks like two things. Some people see one picture, while others see something different. This is because the brain cannot always **process both pictures** at once, or even at all.

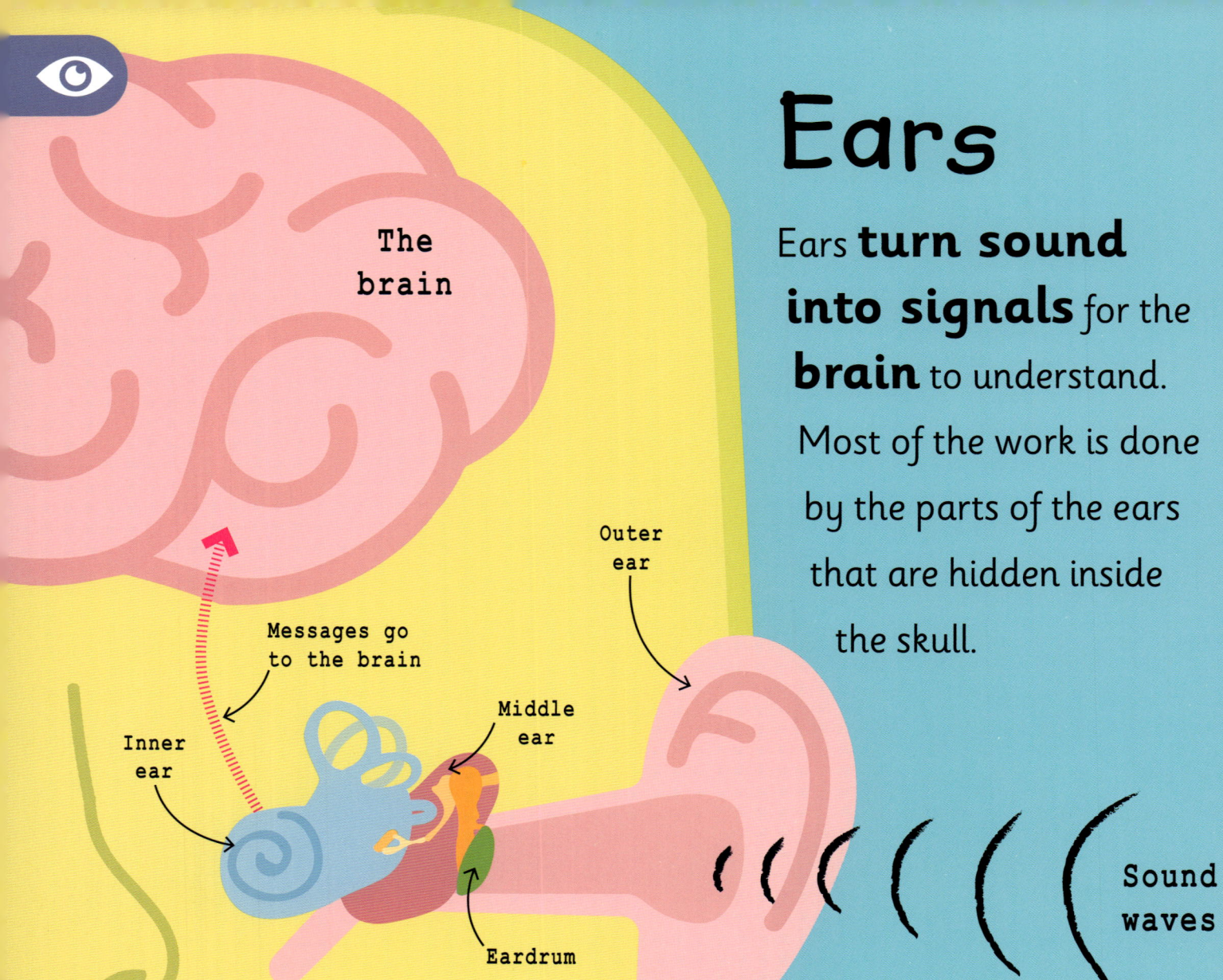

Ears

Ears **turn sound into signals** for the **brain** to understand. Most of the work is done by the parts of the ears that are hidden inside the skull.

The brain

Messages go to the brain

Inner ear

Middle ear

Outer ear

Eardrum

Sound waves

Good vibrations
The outer ear **collects** sounds. As sound travels inside the ear, parts of the ear vibrate. The information about these vibrations travels to the **brain**, to help it work out the noise.

Beat of the drum
Sounds hit a thin layer of skin, called the **eardrum**, and make it vibrate — just like a real drum. The eardrum protects the inside of the ear.

The bones in the middle ear are the TINIEST BONES in the body.

Small hearing aid

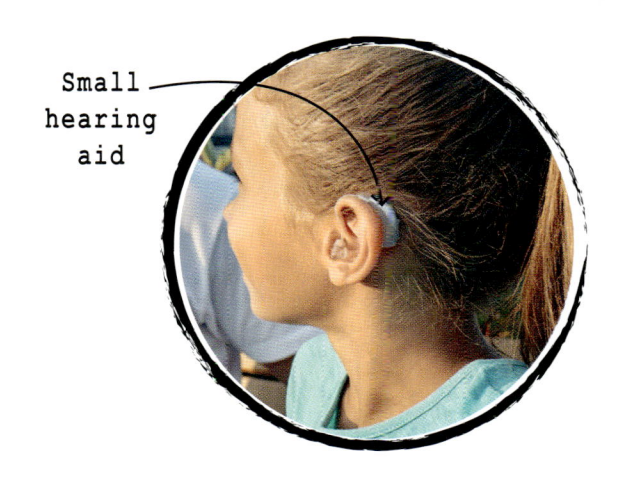

Hearing levels
Some people **have trouble hearing**, or may not be able to hear at all. They might use a hearing aid. It is also common for hearing to get worse as people get **older**.

Speak up! I'm a bit hard of hearing.

In the past, if someone was **hard of hearing** they would use a **big trumpet** to collect sounds. It acted like a bigger version of the **outer ear**.

Animal ears
An animal's sense of hearing **helps it survive** in its environment, so each animal has ears that suit its home and **lifestyle**. Some animals can also use their ears for other things.

Bats need big ears because they have weaker eyesight and rely on their hearing.

Bat

Fennec fox

Fennec foxes have big ears that help keep themselves cool in the hot desert.

Some dogs have extra muscles in their ears so they can move them around to locate sounds.

Dog

Hoooowwwl!

131

Ear-splitting sounds

Sounds vary in how **loud** or **soft** they are. Loudness is measured in **decibels** (dB). Very loud sounds can hurt the ears, so be careful when listening to **loud noises**.

Fireworks

Whispering — 30dB

Talking — 65dB

Busy traffic — 80dB

Baby crying — 110dB

Thunder — 120dB

140dB

Decibels

The human ear can **safely** hear sounds up to 80dB, such as **busy traffic**, or a noisy room full of people. Listening to louder sounds is fine in **small bursts**, but doing it for a long time can cause **damage** to our ears.

The loudest natural sound on Earth was made by an erupting volcano.

Pitch

Pitch is another way to measure sound. **High-pitched sounds** are squeaky and shrill, like a **bird chirping**. **Low-pitched sounds** are soft and quiet, like the **rumble of thunder**. Pitch is measured in hertz (Hz).

Sensing sounds

It's possible for deaf people, who can't hear, to **sense sound** through **vibrations** in the ground. This means they can **dance** or **play instruments**, even if they can't hear music in the typical way.

Evelyn Glennie is a percussionist who is deaf. She plays barefoot so that she can feel the vibrations on stage as she performs with an orchestra.

Animal power

Many animals have a greater **hearing range** than humans. **Dogs** can hear very **high-pitched** sounds that humans can't detect. And **bats** have an even greater hearing range!

I can hear higher-pitched sounds than dogs can. I can hear mice squeaking!

The eyes, brain, muscles, and skin sensors help to keep us from falling over.

Keeping your balance

Ears aren't just for hearing sounds — they also help with balance. The parts in the **inner ear** helps all this happen without us even knowing it.

Move it

There is special **fluid** and **microscopic (tiny) hairs** inside the ear. They move as you move, sending **information** to the brain to tell it how the body is positioned.

Motion sickness is very common. This happens when the brain has trouble processing information around you while you're moving.

If you're staying still, but something big is moving in your field of vision, it can trick your brain into thinking you're moving.

People with ear infections can suffer from dizziness and vertigo (a feeling that the world is spinning).

Nose

A nose looks quite ordinary. But inside, it is a world full of **mucus**, **hairs**, **cartilage**, and **bone**.

Bone

Cartilage

Tip of the nose
The tip of the nose is made of a substance called cartilage, which is **firm but squishy**. This means the nostrils can get bigger to inhale air.

The highest bit of the nose is the bridge. The bridge is hard and rigid because there are bones here.

The human nose can distinguish

Animal noses
Each **species' nose** has adapted (changed) over thousands of years to suit the **animal's needs**.

Star-nosed moles have bad eyesight, so their wide noses help them **smell** their way to food.

Stopping dirt

The nose stays clean with the help of **hair** and **mucus** (snot)!

Mucus traps dirt, and keeps the inside of the nose moist. When mucus dries, it becomes a lump called a bogey.

The hairs inside the nose also trap dirt, stopping it from getting into the lungs.

Droopy nose

You might notice that older people have larger noses. This is because **cartilage grows softer** through life, making the nose droop and **look bigger**.

The nostrils can widen as you get older. This means your nose can change shape as you age.

up to 1 TRILLION DIFFERENT SMELLS.

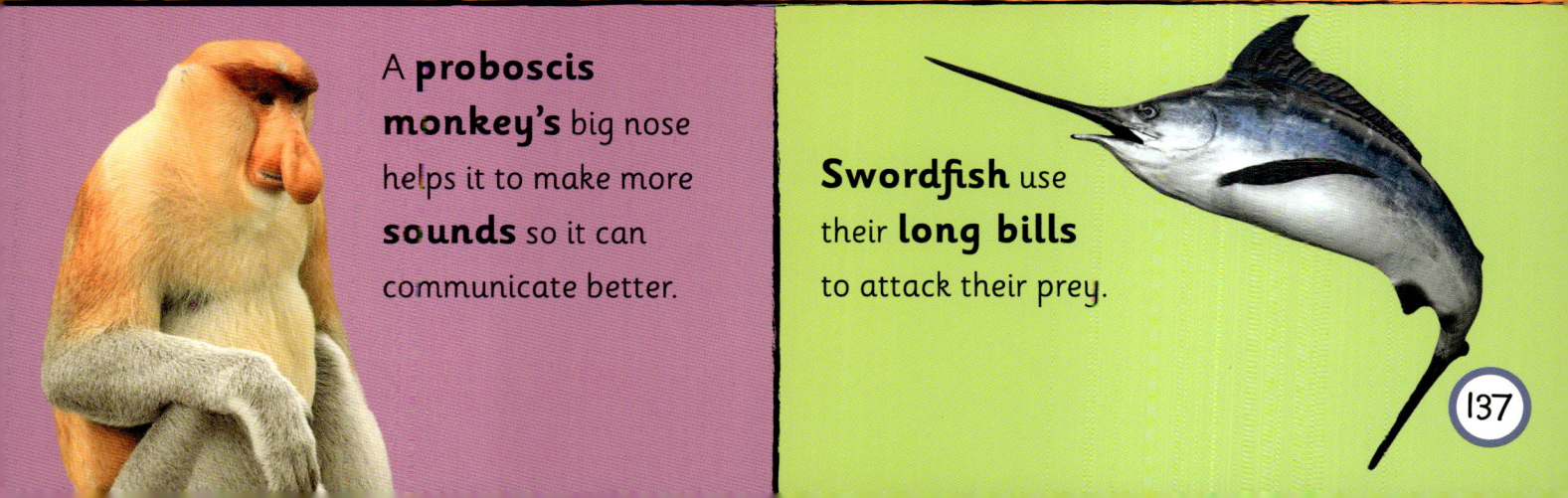

A **proboscis monkey's** big nose helps it to make more **sounds** so it can communicate better.

Swordfish use their **long bills** to attack their prey.

On the scent

The nose collects all **types of smells**. Smells can give clues about the environment around us. Bad smells can tell us if food is **rotting**, which helps us to stay safe.

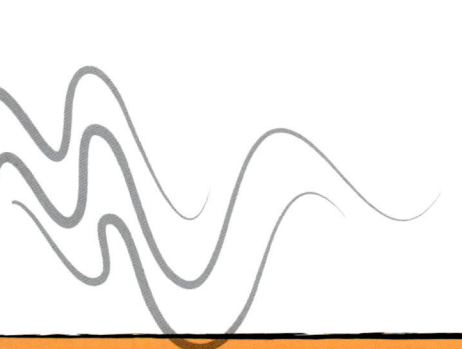

Receptors

Particles

Smell particles bounce around inside the nose, turning on the smell receptors.

What is a smell?
A **smell** is made up of little particles — tiny parts of a solid, liquid, or gas. They enter the nose when you breathe in.

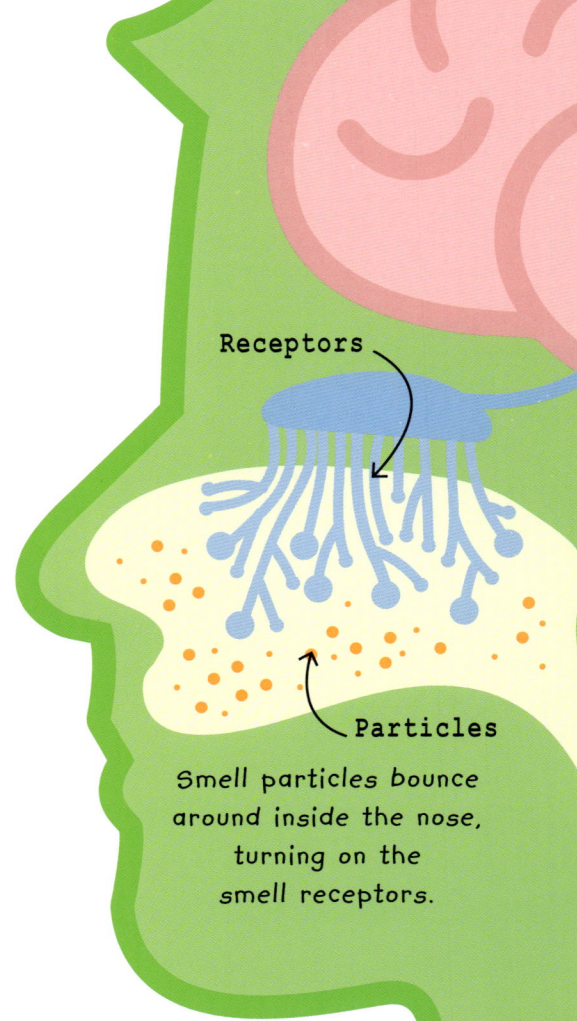

Many animals have AMAZING

A **shark** can detect **one drop of blood** in an area of ocean as **big** as a **swimming pool**.

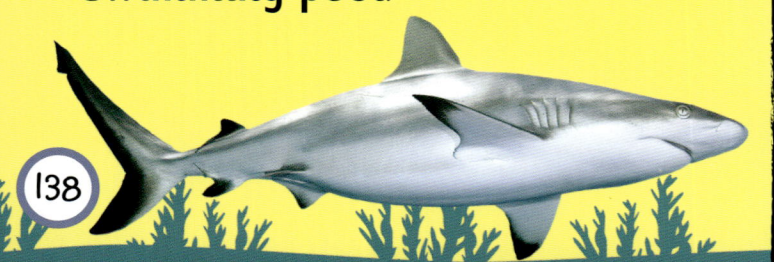

Bloodhounds, a breed of dog, can **track smells** almost **two weeks** after the smell has disappeared!

The brain then works out whether the smell is sweet or nasty!

← Brain

Smell receptors look like hairs but they're actually parts of the nose cells. They convert the smell information into an electrical signal and send it to the brain.

Smelling smelly smells

Special smell **sensors** called receptors live high up inside the nose. One sensor might recognize **nice** smells, and another might detect **stinky** smells.

SMELLING ABILITIES.

Elephants have a sensitive sense of smell. They can **detect** water from **19 km** (12 miles) **away**.

Cows can smell things **8 km** (5 miles) **away**, which helps to keep them safe from danger.

Touch

When a person touches something, **information** is sent to the **brain** about whether it feels **hot** or **cold**, **scratchy** or **soft**.

Brain

From fingertip to brain
There are thousands of **sense receptors** on the skin. Receptors are tiny parts of the body that **receive information** about its surroundings, and send that information quickly to the brain. Even if a person **touches** something lightly, the receptors still detect how something feels.

Reading by touch

Braille is a type of **language** designed for people who are visually impaired. People move their fingertips over a series of **dots** that form **letters**, **words**, and **sentences**.

Too much information

The brain receives lots of information all the time, but it will try to **focus on things that are important**, like pain. This can help keep you safe.

What information will the brain focus on here?

The feel of the breeze

Sudden pain

Ouch!

The ground underneath

The feeling of fabric

Insect senses

Insects feel the world through their **antennae**. These are found on their heads and are used for **touch** and **smell**.

Antennae

141

Tip of the tongue

The tongue is a **muscle** that helps to break down food. It also has thousands of **tiny bumps** on its surface that help with **taste**.

> Information from the taste buds is turned into electrical signals and sent to the brain.

Taste buds
Taste buds are found all over the tongue. These little bumps **detect** taste through **taste pores** (tiny holes in the skin).

Taste buds

> There could be up to 4,000 taste buds in the mouth.

How many?
The number of **taste buds** on the tongue varies. This is why people experience different taste **sensations**.

Super tasters

Super tasters can **detect flavours** very well. They are able to taste the **smallest hint of flavour** in foods.

Broccoli tastes especially bitter for super tasters!

Tasteful
It was once thought that different parts of the tongue had specific taste buds – so one part could detect **bitterness**, and one part could detect **sweetness**. Now we know that's false.

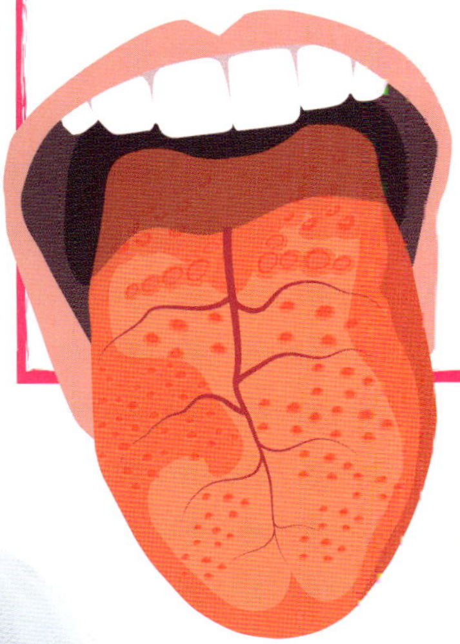

Taste buds detecting the five basic flavours are found all over the tongue.

Sensational
A study found that **girls** have a **stronger sense** of taste than **boys**. Both had the same number of taste buds, but their taste sensations were different!

Mouthwatering
As well as the main tastes, some foods create a hot or cold feeling on the tongue. Eating a hot chilli is a different sensation to eating cooling cucumber!

Taste

There are **five basic tastes**. These are sour, bitter, salty, sweet, and umami. Which one is your **favourite?**

Sour
Foods like **lemons** and natural **yoghurt** have a sour taste. When eating them, the **salivary glands** in the mouth spring into action to make lots of saliva to help digest them.

The more red or ripe the strawberry is, the sweeter it will taste!

Sweet
Some **fruits** have a **natural sweet** taste. Foods with **added sugar** like **cupcakes** also taste sweet.

Many foods have SUGAR ADDED to them,

Bitter

Bitter tastes come from foods like **broccoli**, **kale**, **cabbages**, and **grapefruit**. They contain chemicals that make them taste bitter. These types of foods are important for a healthy diet.

Salty

Foods that taste salty include **cheese** and **crisps**. Some of these foods aren't naturally salty — they have salt added to them.

Umami

Umami is the savoury, **meaty taste** found in things like **tomatoes**, **meat**, **mushrooms**, and **fish**. It is also found in **edible seaweed**. Adding an umami taste can make food even yummier.

Taste buds get weaker as we age, so we're less sensitive to taste. If there's a food you don't like, it's worth trying it again in the future. You may find you like it a lot more!

so be careful how many sweet things you eat.

Yummy or yucky?

The **brain** decides whether food tastes good or bad by using several senses all together: **touch**, **smell**, **vision**, and **taste**. If something doesn't feel, smell, or look good, it can be hard to believe it will taste good!

Feels warm!

Smells fishy!

Looks colourful!

Looking good
Colourful foods that have different textures, tastes, and smells are very appealing. The **senses work together** to help bring out the full flavour of the food.

Looks boring!

Looks tempting!

Working together

Before we eat something, the brain processes the **sight and smell** of the food to try to figure out if it is delicious or disgusting. But the brain's guesses may be wrong, so try new foods and discover how they really taste!

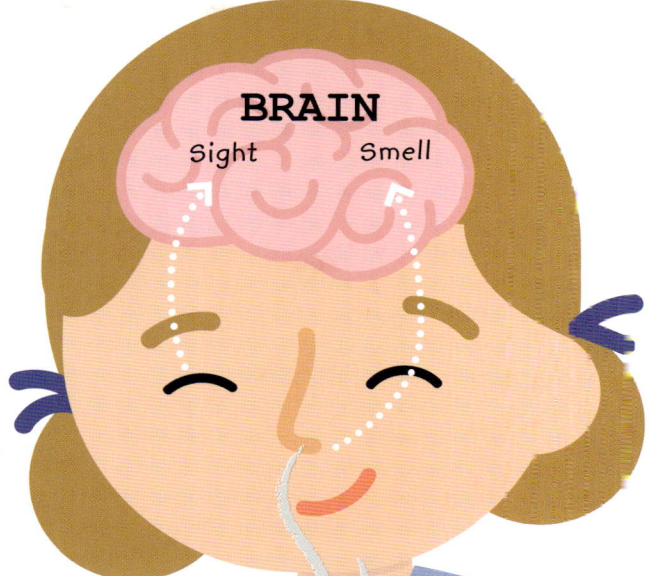

BRAIN
Sight   Smell

Smells yucky!

Smells yummy!

The texture of the food can also play a part in taste.

Smell particles can't travel through a blocked nose, so taste is weaker.

Loss of taste

If the sense of smell **isn't working** properly, food isn't as tasty. This is why people who have a cold and can't smell **go off their food**.

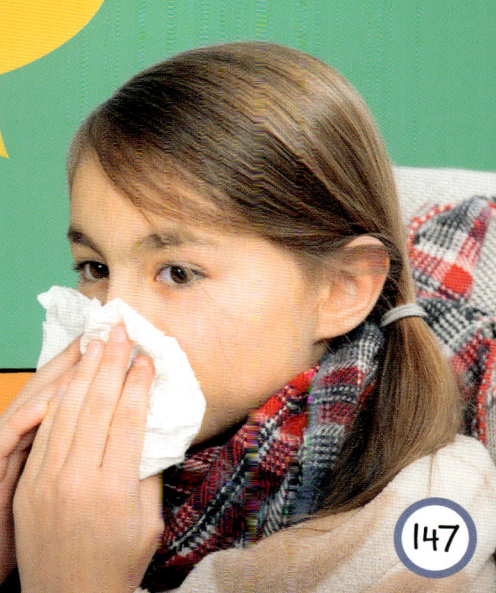

80 per cent of food's taste comes from its smell!

147

More marvellous senses

Some people have **more than** the **five main senses**. Not everyone has all these extra senses, or feels them in the same way, but these are some different ways that people can experience the world.

About two per cent of people experience synaesthesia, which is usually genetic (passed on through families).

Unique experiences
We all **experience** our bodies and surroundings **differently**. Noise that can be just right for you might sound too loud for someone else. Some people like squeezy hugs and some prefer a gentle high five.

Inside sense
We know when we're hungry, or thirsty, or need to use the toilet. This is because of **interoception**: the sense of what is going on in the body. This is reported to the brain so we can do what we need to do.

Mixing senses
People who have **synaesthesia** have senses that mix together. For example, they might hear colours, taste shapes, or smell words. If you think of the number 3, does it have a colour or smell or flavour in your mind?

Mmm! This music tastes like strawberries!

Making sense
Everyone recognizes that there are **five main senses**: sight, hearing, smell, touch, and taste. But there are more senses that help us understand our world and our place within it. These extra senses have long names, but don't worry — they are not difficult to understand.

Sixth sense
The sixth sense is not a real sense. It describes the way we might feel like when we know something, without understanding how we know it! Your brain is always picking up on information that you don't even notice, and it helps you to form an opinion.

Balancing act
Can you touch your nose with your eyes shut, or do a cartwheel? **Proprioception** is a sense that helps us to balance. It tells the brain how the body fits into the space around it, where the body parts are, and how they are moving.

Sometimes, when a person loses an arm or leg, they can still sense the missing part. This may be caused by proprioception.

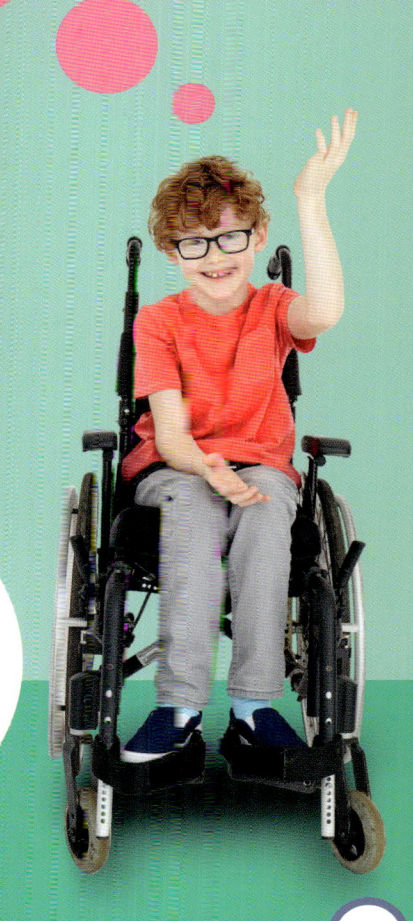

What's going on?

150

Bumps, bruises, and bad germs can leave you feeling hurt or sick. Let's sneak a peek inside the body to discover what's really happening when you're not feeling your best. Luckily, most injuries and illnesses repair with time, or with the help of a doctor. The best thing we can all do is to try and **take care of our bodies** as well as we can.

Early experts

Long before X-rays and cameras helped us see inside the body, **scientists** such as Hippocrates and Abu Bakr al-Razi were making discoveries about **human biology**.

Hippocrates cured the King of Macedonia of the lung disease tuberculosis.

Hippocrates
Greek doctor Hippocrates realized that **diseases had natural causes** and could be cured. He kept notes of patients' symptoms to help diagnose and treat them.

Magic or medicine?
Thousands of years ago in ancient Greece, people didn't understand medicine. They had **superstitious ideas** (believing in magic and luck). They thought that diseases were sent from the gods or **bad spirits**.

Hippocrates was thought to be related to the Greek hero Hercules!

Abu Bakr al-Razi

The greatest doctor and surgeon in the ancient **Arabic world** was Abu Bakr al-Razi. Born in Persia (now Iran) during the **9th century**, he learned about medicine by working at different hospitals.

Abu Bakr al-Razi was among the first to realize that healthy food could help patients feel better.

Medical masterpieces

Abu Bakr al-Razi wrote down everything he learned in more than **200 books**. He wrote *Al-Hawi fi al-Tibb*, the **biggest medical encyclopaedia**, at 23 books long. It included the **medical histories** of various countries, and al-Razi's own medical theories. Sadly, there are no copies left in the world.

Abu Bakr al-Razi practised alchemy: trying to turn ordinary metals into glittering gold!

Head lice

Head lice are **little bugs** that set up home in your hair. They feast on tiny amounts of your blood, and make your head feel itchy. **Yuck!**

The bugs bite into the scalp to feed on blood. This is what makes your head feel so itchy.

Hairy hold
A **head louse** is only the size of a sugar granule. Seen under a microscope, it has **six legs with claws to grip tightly onto hair**.

Bad eggs

Female head lice produce about **five eggs a day**. In just over a week, they hatch as more **blood-sucking head lice**!

These egg cases (nits) look like tiny white specks in the hair close to the scalp.

Classroom critters

Children are most likely to get head lice at **school**. Lice can jump from head to head when people come into **close contact** with each other.

Bug removal

Before you start, you'll need to get a special nit comb designed to remove the bugs.

- First, wash your hair using shampoo and conditioner.
- Ask an adult to comb through your hair. This takes time, so be patient.
- If this doesn't work, chemical shampoos can get rid of nits.

Nit comb

Temperature rising

If you're soaked with sweat and hot to the touch, you may have a **fever**. A high temperature can be a sign of **infection**.

Just right
A **normal temperature** for children is around **37°C (98.6°F)** and the body works hard to keep it at this level.

A fever is when your temperature is 38°C (100°F) or higher.

Wow! Too hot for me!

Hot and bothered
Fevers can be uncomfortable but they help **fight infections**, including colds, flu, tonsillitis, and chickenpox. High temperatures make it hard for bacteria and viruses to survive in the body.

Measuring temperature

It is useful to have a thermometer at home for measuring body temperature. Some thermometers are placed under the **armpit** or in the **mouth** or **ear**, and infrared thermometers scan the **forehead**.

37.5

Infrared thermometer

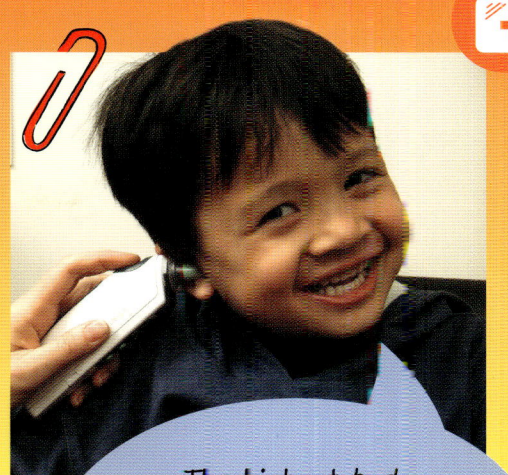

The highest body temperature ever known was 46°C (115°F). This was recorded in a man who had heatstroke, not a fever.

Fighting fevers

As the body is hotter, it is important to drink more, to replace the **sweat lost**.

Rest and **keep cool** under a sheet until your temperature returns to normal. If you have an infection, you may need antibiotics (medicines that fight bacteria).

A raised temperature can sometimes mean a person has something more than a fever, and they may need to see a doctor.

Hatching time

Temperature affects whether newborn crocodiles are **boys or girls**. A temperature of 32°C (90°F) brings a boy, while less than 31°C (88°F) or more than 33°C (91°F) brings a girl!

157

Busy bedtime

The brain doesn't **switch off** completely while you sleep, so nighttime can be a surprisingly busy time!

Sweet dreams

Everyone has dreams — even if they don't remember them. It happens when the **brain becomes more active** in the sleep cycle. The average person has nearly **2,000 dreams** a year.

In control

Lucid dreaming is very rare, but some people claim to experience it often. This is when you **realize you're dreaming**, and you can **change the events** going on in your dream!

Some people think dreams have meanings. For example, having a dream about flying means you're happy.

Sleepwalking isn't dangerous. But it's best to guide a sleepwalker back to bed or wake them up, so that they don't accidentally get hurt.

Up and about

Sometimes when **shifting between stages** of deep and light sleep, the body seems to wake up, but the brain doesn't. People may **walk, talk,** and even do **common tasks** in their sleep. They don't usually remember what they've done.

Animals also dream!

It's thought that animals dream about everyday things, like running and playing.

Sleepwalking and sleeptalking are more common in children than adults.

159

Fight, flight, or freeze?

Long ago, humans needed to survive in the wild. Sometimes they ran into **danger**, so their bodies developed **instincts** (feelings) to protect them. We still have these instincts today.

High alert
When faced with danger, the body has three choices: **face** the threat (fight), **run away** (flight), or **wait** until the danger passes (freeze).

These REACTIONS don't only happen when you're in danger. They can also happen when you're being chased FOR FUN in a game of tag.

Adrenaline rush
A hormone called adrenaline enters the bloodstream to prepare your body for action.

Fully focused
The eyes widen and the pupils get bigger. This makes it easier to see clearly.

Beating heart
The heart beats faster, sending a rush of blood to the muscles to give the body energy.

Deep breath
The airways open wider to allow more air into the lungs.

Emotional reactions
All these physical feelings in the body, and the worry from the stress, can make a person cry, get angry, or feel brave!

These changes happen so quickly in the body that the brain can't always choose how to react. Instead, the body decides whether to face the danger, run away, or freeze up.

Extreme excitement

Adrenaline is not just produced in threatening situations. It can also happen because of **stress**, like during a test at school, or because of **excitement**, like when a person is skydiving.

Queasy feeling
The adrenaline may make the body start to sweat, or make the tummy feel wobbly.

Calming down
Once the stress has passed, a person might still feel nervous from the adrenaline. Playing a game or doing breathing exercises can help them feel better.

Stuck in a state
There are some medical conditions that cause the body to be stuck in the "fight, flight, or freeze" state. If this happens to somebody, they will need treatment to help them manage it.

Coughs and sneezes

Coughs and sneezes really do **spread diseases**. Both send thousands of **germ-ridden droplets** into the air ready to infect more people.

Coughing
People cough when germs, smoke, dust, or food **irritate the airways**. The body responds by blasting air out of the mouth to clear the **blockage** or **irritation**.

much faster

Cover your mouth with your arm when you cough and sneeze into a tissue so you don't infect other people.

Is it true that if you sneeze with your eyes open, your eyeballs will pop out?

162 About 20 per cent of people SNEEZE IN BRIGHT LIGHT.

Day 976

Donna Griffiths holds the record for the world's longest sneezing fit. She sneezed for 976 days (nearly three years!), and sneezed about one million times in the first year!

Sneezing

Sneezing is an **automatic reaction** you usually can't control. Pollen, dust, or bacteria irritate the nose's **sticky lining**. The body sneezes them out to clear the nostrils.

When a person is asleep, the nerves that cause sneezing are also asleep.

Ah-chooooo!

A sneeze can reach super speeds of **160 KPH (100 MPH)** - than a car on a motorway.

This is false! The eyelids shut automatically when you sneeze. Even if you tried really hard to keep them open, your eyeballs would stay in place. Phew!

This condition is called photic sneezing.

Germs on the go

The world is full of **tiny organisms** (living things also known as microbes) that are too small to see. Some are good for our bodies, but others – **germs** – can cause diseases. The body can kill them off, but there are also lots of ways to help **stop the spread** of germs.

How germs spread
Watery droplets are released from the nose or mouth when you **cough** and **sneeze**. These can contain germs that enter the air and can spread if people touch them or breathe them in.

You can help STOP GERMS SPREADING

Wash your hands regularly, especially after using the toilet and before eating.

Serious diseases

Many germs cause mild diseases such as **colds** or **sore throats**, which get better with rest. Other diseases are more serious and may need medical attention.

The immune system attacks bacteria and viruses to protect the body.

Unwelcome visitors

The most common types of germs are **bacteria** and **viruses**. Although small, they can cause infections and make people **feel ill** when they enter the human body.

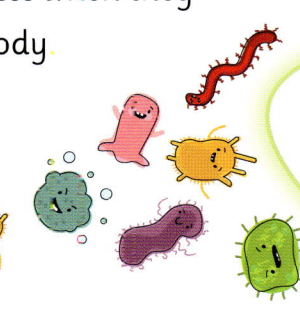

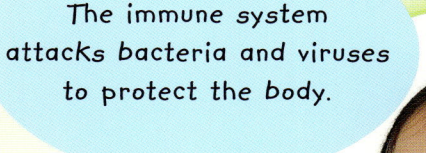

by KEEPING CLEAN.

Cover your mouth with your arm when you cough or sneeze, or use a tissue. If you cough or sneeze into your hand, it will be covered in germs that could spread when you touch things.

Germs can't survive on surfaces for very long, but it's still important to keep things clean to get rid of germs.

Victorious vaccines

The invention of vaccines has helped to keep people across the world **safe from certain diseases**. Sometimes they can get rid of some diseases completely.

How a vaccine works

Vaccines teach the immune system in the body how to **fight off germs**. The immune system can then recognize and destroy those germs if it comes into contact with them in the future.

In the 1700s, the smallpox virus killed about 400,000 people a year. An English doctor named Edward Jenner noticed that some farmers caught a milder version of the disease, called cowpox. These people then became immune to smallpox.

First vaccine

In 1796, Dr Edward Jenner created a **vaccine for smallpox** using the milder version of the disease, cowpox. This was the world's first widely used vaccine.

Global spread

History has had its share of diseases. They can start from **epidemics** in smaller communities, and grow into **pandemics** that spread to multiple countries. But scientists can **create vaccines** that help to protect our bodies from these germs.

The Plague was a disease caused by bacteria from flea bites. It killed 50 million people in the mid-1300s.

Rat fleas carried the Plague.

The **COVID-19** pandemic began in late 2019. Within a year, scientists had developed a vaccine that helped to protect the body from the most serious effects of the virus.

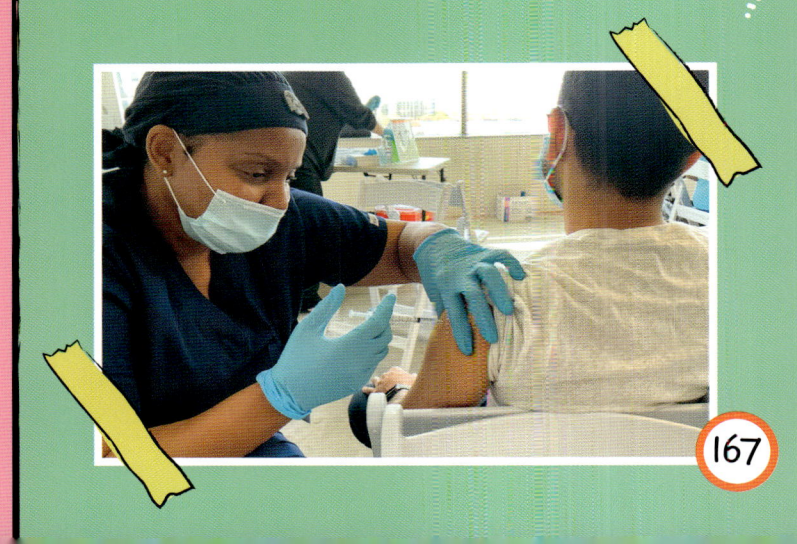

A severe strain of flu, known as **Spanish flu**, wiped out three per cent of the world's population in 1918.

Aaah aaaah ah-choooo!

All about allergies

Your body systems are hard at work **protecting** you. But sometimes the smallest and most surprising things cause a big **reaction** inside the body…

Allergens
Substances that cause **allergic reactions** are called allergens. Here are some examples.

Animals
Some people are allergic to **animal hairs**. They have to take care around some pets.

Dust
For some people, **small bugs** that live in dust can cause sneezing, sore eyes, or a runny nose.

Allergic reactions can be very dangerous. They can make it hard to breathe so the person might need to go to hospital.

Allergic reactions

The immune system protects the body by reacting to **harmful germs**. But if it reacts to something that is usually harmless, it can **cause a response** called an allergic reaction.

Allergy protection

There is no real cure for allergies, so people with allergies should try to **avoid getting close** to any allergens. If they do have a mild reaction, this can be treated with **medicines**.

Mild reactions

Some allergic reactions are mild, causing only swelling and soreness. **Coughing**, **sneezing**, and **irritated skin or eyes** are typical.

Serious reactions

For serious reactions, some people use a special injection that **pumps adrenaline** into the body. It's only used in emergencies.

Food

Foods, including **peanuts**, **shellfish**, and **dairy products**, can produce an allergic reaction.

Insect stings

Some people are allergic to **bee** or **wasp stings**. They can make it hard to breathe properly.

Medicine

Some people cannot have **certain medicines** because they can cause rashes, swellings, or breathing issues.

169

Hay fever season

Summertime means **sneezy time** for many. **Warm weather** marks the start of hay fever season. Luckily, there are things you can do to feel better.

Plant pollen
Pollen is a **dusty powder** produced by grass, trees, and flowers. There is more pollen in the air on **dry, hot days**, and even more on **windy days**. This can be difficult for people with hay fever.

Pollen in the air

Pollen

170

People with hay fever can check the pollen count online. The higher the pollen count, the more pollen grains in the air, and the greater the chance of hay fever symptoms.

Asthma attack

Allergies like hay fever can trigger a breathing problem called **asthma**. This makes it hard to breathe. People with asthma can use an **inhaler** if they have an asthma attack.

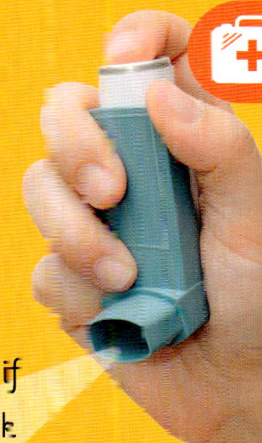

An **allergy** to plant pollen is called hay fever. Symptoms include a **runny nose**, **itchy throat**, **tickly cough**, **watery eyes**, and **sneezing**.

Top tips

Here are the best ways to fight hay fever:

- Wear sunglasses to prevent pollen entering your eyes.
- Wash your hands regularly if you can't help rubbing your eyes.
- Stay indoors if possible when the pollen count is high.
- Keep bedroom windows and doors closed at night.
- Pollen sticks to clothes, so shower or wash after school and put on clean clothes.
- Rub moisturiser around your nose to ease the soreness.
- Antihistamine is a medicine that you can buy from the chemist to help hay fever symptoms.

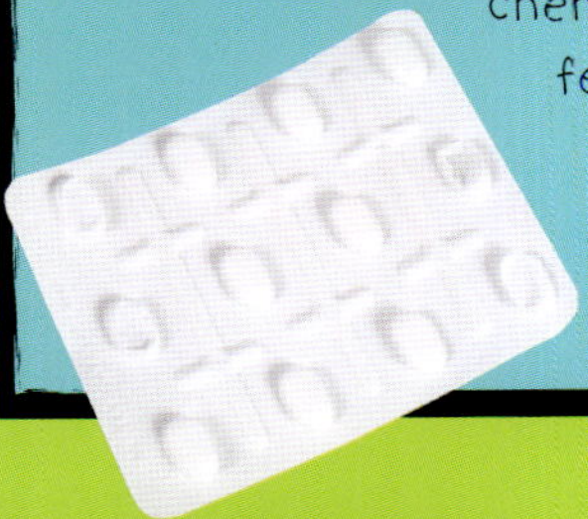

Good news!

Most people with hay fever find the **symptoms get better** as they get older — and can stop altogether in about 20 per cent of cases.

Down the wrong way

Have you ever **swallowed** something that went down the wrong way? This happens when your food or drink takes a **wrong turn** and goes down a different tube.

Food travels down the oesophagus

Air travels down the windpipe

Stomach

Lungs

Inside the body
Two tubes lead down from your throat. Food and drink is pushed down into one tube – the **oesophagus** – on its way to the stomach. Air is taken in through the other tube – the **windpipe** – to the lungs.

The journey from the mouth to the stomach takes only seven seconds.

When food goes down the WRONG TUBE it is coughed out FAST!

Food flap
A small flap at the **back of the throat** closes over the windpipe to **stop food or drink** getting into it every time the body swallows.

Occasionally the flap in the throat can fail, letting food, drink, or saliva slip past it and enter the windpipe instead. This can create a blockage inside the airways and you may start choking.

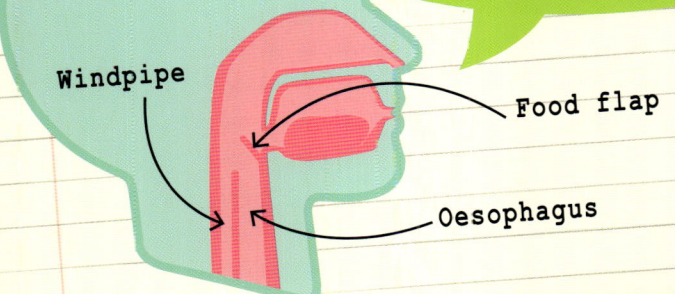

Windpipe
Food flap
Oesophagus

Coughing fit
If you have a **blockage**, your body responds with a series of **big coughs** to clear it. The force of the coughing sends the swallowed food or drink flying up the **windpipe** and out of the mouth. Then your breathing will return to normal.

Sore throat
Children often get sore throats. Most are caused by **viruses**. If your throat is sore, **drink lots of water**, eat soft foods, and get lots of sleep. It should go away in a few days.

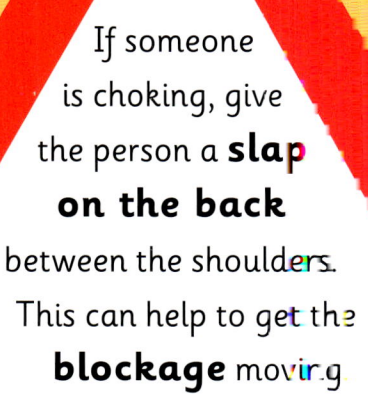

If someone is choking, give the person a **slap on the back** between the shoulders. This can help to get the **blockage** moving

WARNING!

Tummy pains

Most people know that horrible feeling of a **churning tummy** before you're sick. Let's look at what might be going on inside of you.

Feeling sick

You can feel ill for a **variety of reasons**, including:

Eating so much your tummy becomes overstretched.

A virus you've come into contact with.

Food poisoning from something that wasn't cooked properly or was out of date.

Motion sickness from travelling.

174

Some people cannot process certain foods without **feeling sick**.

Feeling worried or nervous about something.

Michel Lotito had the strongest of stomachs. Despite swallowing glass, metal, and rubber, he was never sick. Lotito chomped his way through bicycles, shopping trolleys, and a small plane. Do not try this at home!

Tummy trouble
Usually the stomach is a happy place, full of food to keep the body fit and healthy. But if the **lining of the tummy** becomes irritated, you can feel sick.

Signs of sickness
Extra **saliva** is produced and you break into a sweat. You start to feel like you might be sick. Tummy muscles begin moving and the **body starts to heave**.

Up and out!
The body's automatic reaction is **to be sick**, and it can't stop. Sick flies up the oesophagus and out of the mouth.

Sick is always better out than in. Once the problem has cleared, the tummy usually calms down. It's a good idea to sip water, have a sleep, and wait several hours before eating.

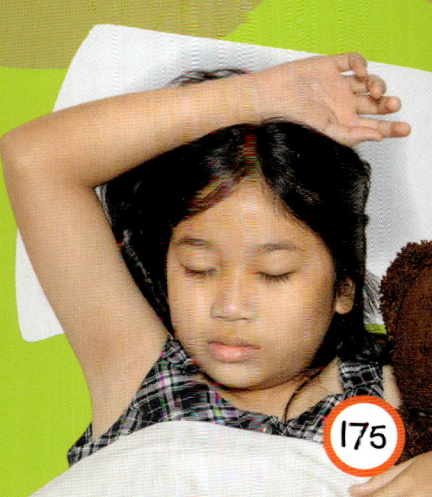

Sun safety

Bright sunshine and **blue skies** can cheer us up and make people feel **happy**. However, the sun can be **harmful**, so avoid having too much of a good thing!

Suncream
Be careful – everyone can get sunburn, regardless of their skin tone. This is why it is important to use **suncream**. Use SPF (Sun Protection Factor) 50 for the highest protection.

Vitamin D
Sunlight produces vitamin D in the skin. This vitamin is good for you in all kinds of ways. It helps the body absorb **calcium** from food to keep **bones** and **teeth healthy**. Many people take extra vitamin D tablets.

Sunburn

Sunburn makes skin feel **sore**. Most importantly, **ultraviolet** (UV) rays in sunlight can **damage skin cells** and lead to health conditions in the future, so be careful in the sun.

Sunstroke

Too much time in the sun can be dangerous. Heat exhaustion causes **headaches**, **sickness**, and **dizziness**. This can lead to sunstroke and hospital treatment.

Top tips

Here is your checklist for when the heat is on

- Find a shady spot if the heat is too strong.
- Avoid the sun during the hottest time of the day.
- Drink lots of water to keep cool.
- Wear light, loose clothing.
- Wear sunglasses and a sun hat.
- Reapply suncream regularly, especially after swimming.
- Avoid leaving pets in the car on hot days, even with a window open.

Sore stings

Bees are very **hard workers** and do lots of jobs. If a bee is **scared**, it can **sting** a human. It is the bee's way of saying "**Leave me alone**"!

Bees sting to defend themselves against a threat.

Hard at work
Bees visit plants to **gather food**. That's why there are often bees around when we go out to a **park** or **playground** where there are lots of plants and flowers.

Bees do a SPECIAL DANCE to let other

Warning!
A bee's body has a **sharp stinger**. When it feels **threatened**, it puts its stinger into the attacker. The stinger contains **venom**, which is a mild poison.

One-time use
Wasps can sting **again** and **again**, but bees can't. Bees can only sting once because their **stinger falls off** as soon as it has been used.

Allergies

Someone who is **allergic** to **insect stings** may have a serious reaction to getting stung. They will need immediate **medical care** if they have a serious reaction, such as having breathing problems, **fainting**, or being **sick**.

bees know they've found new flowers.

Ouch!

After a **bee sting**, the area can be painful. The **skin swells** and a red mark is left at the site. This usually **heals** with time.

Medicine

Antihistamines are **medicines** that help swellings go down after a bee sting. They also help **reduce itching** that can occur after a bee sting.

Blood can become trapped, turning into a visible mark that hurts to the touch.

Black and blue

Bruises can turn your skin black and blue – and just about every **shade** of the **rainbow**! But what exactly is a bruise?

Behind the bruise

Any bang, bash, or bump can make its mark on the skin. The impact of the injury causes blood from damaged blood vessels to leak under the skin.

After a week or so, the bruise fades to yellow or green as the blood is absorbed back into the body.

After a day, the bruise really comes out, turning blue or black in some cases.

A bruise looks red or purple in colour when the blood first leaks under the skin.

After about two weeks, the rainbow disappears, leaving your skin like new!

180

Elderly people bruise more easily because their blood vessels are weaker.

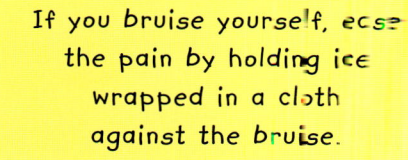

If you bruise yourself, ease the pain by holding ice wrapped in a cloth against the bruise.

People with haemophilia bruise more easily.

Big bruisers
Anyone can bruise, but bruises show more clearly on lighter skin tones. Some people are more likely to bruise if they have **thinner skin**, or have certain medical conditions.

Cool and calm
You can avoid bruises by simply **slowing down**, so accidents are less likely to happen. If you are riding a scooter, skateboard, or bike, wear protective gear such as a helmet, and knee and elbow pads.

Extra caution
Blood clots happen when **blood forms a lump** to stop too much blood from leaking out of a cut. People with the condition haemophilia have blood that doesn't clot well, so they can bleed for longer.

Cuts and scrapes

Ouch! It hurts when the skin is cut open, even if the cut is small. The body can often heal the cut itself. This stops too much blood from escaping and infection getting in.

1

Bleeding cut
Skin is full of blood vessels (tubes that carry blood). When skin is cut, it bleeds because the vessels are damaged.

2

That hurts!
Pain receptors (nerve endings) in the skin are activated when skin is damaged. They send information through the nerves to tell the brain there's a problem!

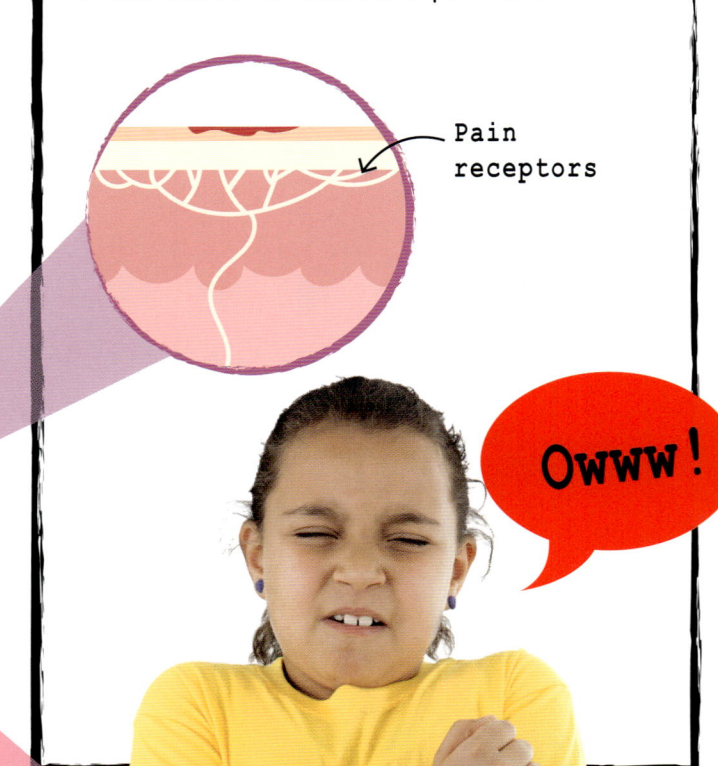

Pain receptors

Owww!

People feel different levels of pain, and some are more sensitive to pain than others.

182

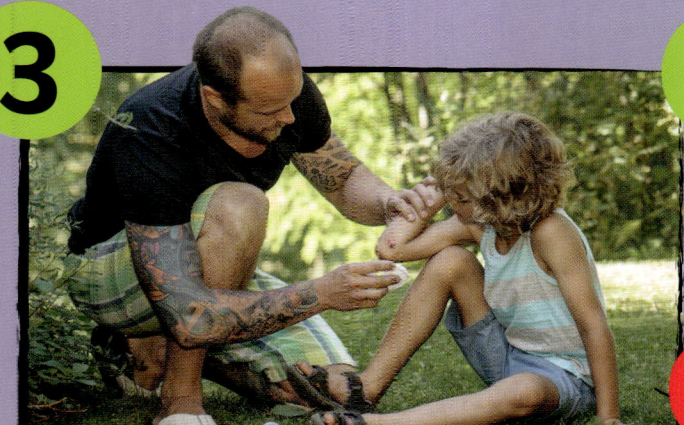

3 Clean up
All cuts must be kept clean to stop infection. Ask an adult to wash the cut with water and apply a plaster or dressing.

4 Keep it in
When skin is cut, platelets rush to the site to form a clot. They make a substance called fibrin that helps to seal the wound.

Platelets
Red cells
White cells
Fibrin

5 Scabbing over
The clot dries out and forms a scab, which is crusty and itchy. Don't pull it off as it keeps the wound safe while the skin heals!

6 All better
The body repairs broken skin. Some cells multiply and form new skin, while white blood cells ensure the infection stays away.

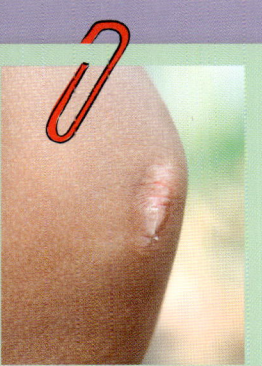

White blood cell

Scars can form where wounds have healed. They come in all shapes and sizes and are clues to old injuries. Scar tissue is weaker than normal skin tissue. Scars tell a story of the times your body healed itself.

In the past, plasters were made from plants, herbs, and mud.

Broken bones

Breaking, or fracturing, a bone can be painful but it can be treated. The bone can **heal on its own**, if the break is kept safe and given some time.

Spongy bone

Some people have a condition where the bones are weak and can break more easily. This is called osteoporosis. The spongy bone interior becomes brittle. There are lots of causes, including genetics, ageing, or a diet lacking in important vitamins.

Swelling and bruising

When a bone fractures or breaks, swelling and bruising appears, and it's painful. That's because **fluid leaks** into places where it's not meant to go!

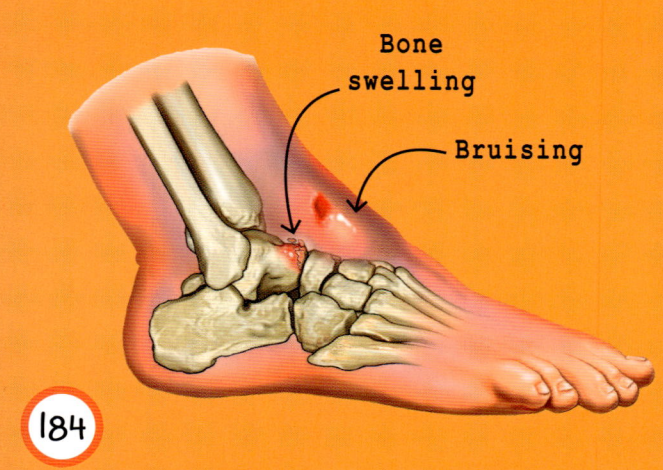

Bone swelling

Bruising

Blood clots

Blood usually clots around the fracture to stop the bleeding. New bone cells are laid down to **fill the gap between the break**. This can take up to 12 weeks.

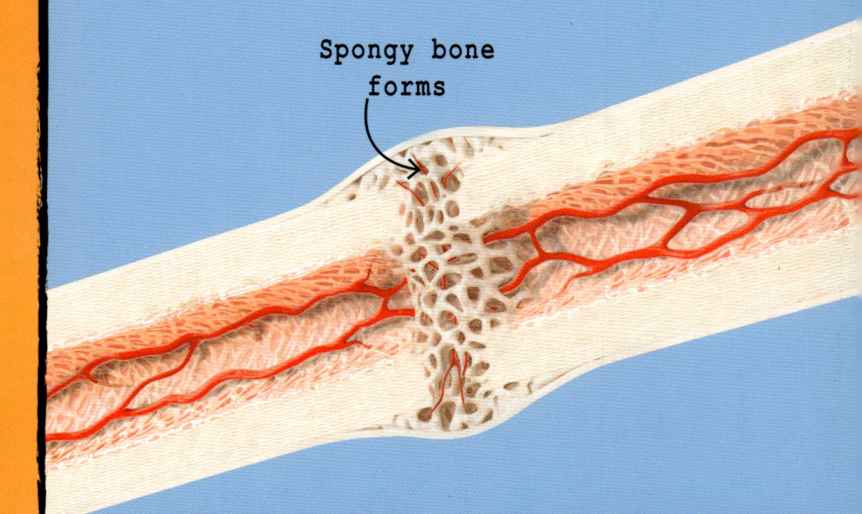

Spongy bone forms

Casting call

If you break a bone, you may need a cast. This is made of bandages, and usually plaster. The rigid cast stops the area around the bone from moving, allowing the break **time to heal**.

Often when people have a cast, they get friends and family to sign it or draw pictures on it!

Helping hand

Sometimes a broken bone can stick out at an angle. Medical help is needed to put the bone back into position. Then a cast is used to **keep the bone in place** as it heals.

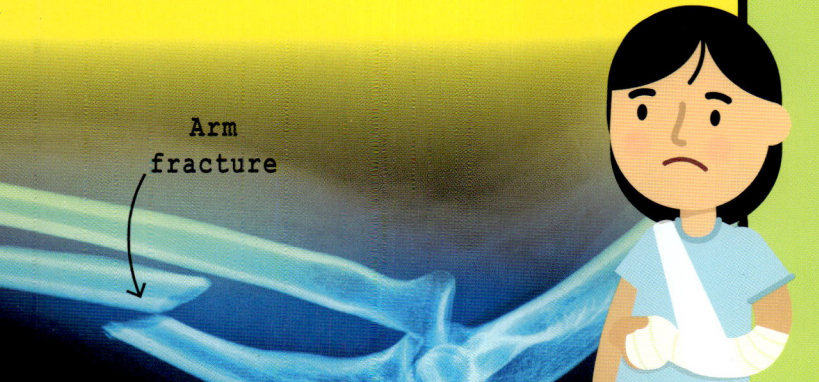

Arm fracture

Greenstick fractures

These fractures are where the bone cracks but doesn't break. They are common in children, as young bones are bendy!

Greenstick arm fracture

185

Lifesaving discoveries

Sometimes all it takes is one **incredible idea** to create a **cure** that saves the lives of millions of people around the world. Just like these...

Accidental antibiotics

Medicine that **fights bacteria**, called antibiotics, have helped people worldwide. But Scottish scientist Sir Alexander Fleming discovered them by accident!

Bacteria and mould under microscope

Mouldy milestone

During the 1920s, Fleming had left some bacteria in his lab. He returned to find the bacteria were surrounded by mould, and he noticed that chemicals in the mould were **killing off the bacteria**.

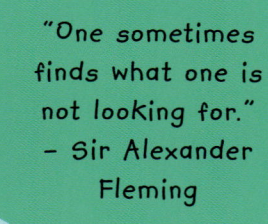

"One sometimes finds what one is not looking for."
– Sir Alexander Fleming

Powerful penicillin

Fleming's discovery led to the development of penicillin, the first antibiotic. It remains a **common treatment** for bacterial infections in the body.

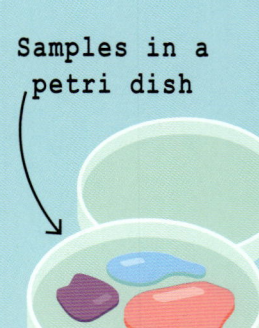

Samples in a petri dish

Both Fleming and Youyou received the

Devastating disease
Chinese chemist Tu Youyou studied the terrible effects of **malaria**. This disease is spread by mosquito bites, and millions of people have died from it.

Sweet wormwood

Plant power
While studying traditional medicines in the 1960s and 70s, Youyou came across the sweet wormwood plant. She realized that it contained chemicals that could **fight off malaria**. Youyou was the first person to trial her own potential malaria treatment.

"Every scientist dreams of doing something that can help the world."
– Tu Youyou

Malaria medicine
Youyou's malaria treatment is used across Asia, Africa, and South America, where malaria affects **millions of people**.

NOBEL PRIZE IN MEDICINE.

Living well

To stay in tip-top condition, you need to **take care of yourself**, both inside and out. Different foods, fun and games, and rest and relaxation all help to keep your body as **strong and healthy** as it can be.

Food for thought

Food is one of life's great pleasures. It makes your tummy happy and your body healthy. A **varied**, **balanced diet** is not only delicious, but essential to keep your body going.

Rumbly tummy
Does your tummy rumble when you're hungry? The intestines below the stomach have air, food, and drink moving through them. When you haven't eaten for a while, these **noises** are **easier to hear** because there is less food **inside** the tummy to dull the sounds.

Full up
An adult's tummy can hold 4 litres (8.5 pints) of food, but this is the limit! When you eat a big meal, your **tummy stretches**. If it feels uncomfortable, you've probably eaten enough!

On average, a person eats about 40 tonnes of food in their lifetime – that's the weight of a sperm whale!

Waste not

About **one third of the food** in the world ends up going in the bin. To help reduce waste, don't put more on your plate than you actually want. You can also try to find out about ways that unwanted food can be used, such as **composting**.

Strong stomach

Your stomach produces a very strong **acid**. This acid must be powerful so that it can **kill bad bacteria** that could enter the body inside food.

Sweets

Many people love the taste of sugary snacks. But make sure not to eat many, or too often. Too much sugar is **bad for your body and teeth**.

Getting to know your food

What are your **favourite foods**? Do you know how they help your body? Different food groups nourish (support) the body in different ways.

Eating veggies with the skins on is better for you. The skin is full of vitamins.

Fruit and vegetables

Vegetables contain fibre, which helps keep the gut working well.

Fruit and vegetables

A healthy diet includes **five** pieces of fruit and vegetables a day. Eating **different coloured** fruit and vegetables helps the body get a good dose of vitamins. It doesn't matter if it's fresh or frozen fruit or veg.

Proteins

Meat, fish, eggs, tofu, nuts, beans, and pulses (such as chickpeas) contain protein. Protein helps **build** and **repair** cells. It's important to eat protein each day.

Different vitamins help with different things. For example, Vitamin A helps eyes see clearly.

Proteins

Try to eat a BALANCED DIET that

Carbohydrates

Foods including rice and pasta are made up of carbohydrates. They give us **energy**. They should make up a third of the plate when you have your main meal of the day.

Carbohydrates

Dairy

The body needs a little bit of fat, too. Fat can be found in many foods, such as oils and cheese.

Plan a meal

Can you think of a yummy meal that contains all these food groups? What would you add to the plate to make sure you have a balanced meal?

Sugar is found naturally in many foods we eat, such as fruit. The body doesn't usually need the extra sugar in biscuits and cakes!

Dairy

Foods made from cow's milk — such as yoghurt — are called dairy products. They contain calcium, which keeps **bones** strong. Alternatives such as oat milk are also good for you.

contains foods from EVERY GROUP.

Excellent exercise

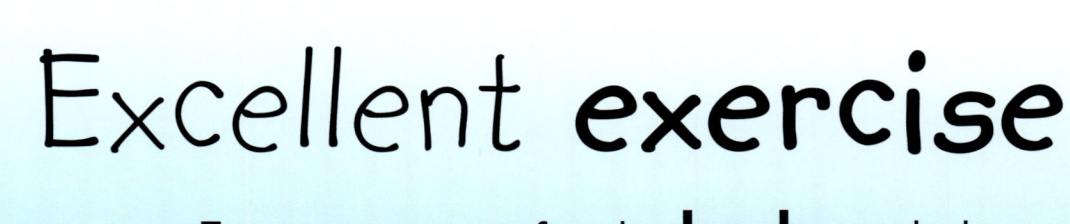

Exercise is great for the **body** and also for the **mind**. It gets blood pumping to muscles and organs, bringing fresh oxygen to all the cells.

Memory can improve if you exercise regularly.

Oats in porridge contain both carbohydrates and protein.

Food

Energy for exercising comes from food. Eating after exercise is also important to **refuel** the body. Your body will need certain nutrients from proteins (found in meat, eggs, and nuts) and carbohydrates (in food such as bread, beans, and pasta).

The benefits of exercise

Boost the blood flow
Organs receive a better blood supply when exercising. This lasts for hours, so exercise **helps your body** work better for a while even after you've stopped moving around!

Exercising can be as simple as playing a sport with your friends.

Blood flow

Staying healthy
Exercising is part of a healthy lifestyle. It helps you **sleep** better, and keeps the body **strong** and **flexible**. Exercising makes the heart beat faster and more strongly for a while, which is good for keeping it healthy.

Muscles
Using your muscles regularly keeps them toned. This means they stay in **good shape**. Muscle cells become larger, and muscles become stronger. Nerve connections between muscles get better, too.

The immune system stays healthy if you exercise regularly. This means you can fight off infections quickly.

Time for bed, sleepyhead

ZZZZzzzzzzzzzzzzzz

A good night's sleep is essential to make sure the body **rests and repairs**. Without it, people can feel exhausted, confused, grumpy, and forgetful. **Night, night! Zzzz...**

Newborn babies sleep for up to 18 hours a day, but this decreases as they get older.

Young children — **12 hours**

Older children — **10 hours**

Adults — **8 hours**

Elderly people — **6 hours**

Can you believe that ONE THIRD of

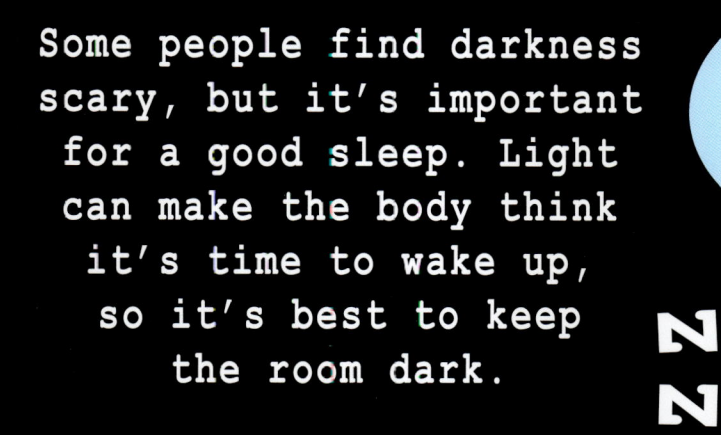

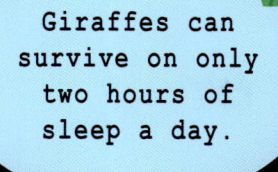

Some people find darkness scary, but it's important for a good sleep. Light can make the body think it's time to wake up, so it's best to keep the room dark.

Giraffes can survive on only two hours of sleep a day.

Koalas sleep for 22 hours a day, as their diet is low in energy. Elephants can survive on just two hours.

Sleep tight

Sleep is just as important for the body as **food** and **water**. Without sleep, the body won't grow as well and the brain works more slowly. That's why it's important to go to bed on time!

Nap time

A **nap during the day** can be good for you, too. It can give you an **energy boost**, and helps your memory work better. Naps are especially important for babies and children.

the average lifetime is SPENT ASLEEP?

Mental health

Mental health affects how we **think**, **feel**, and **act**. It's important to keep our minds healthy, just like all the other parts of the body.

Emotions

It's normal to experience a **range of feelings**. Our thoughts can affect our emotions, and our emotions can affect how we behave. Most people cannot **fully manage** their emotions until adulthood, so sometimes we can have emotional reactions that don't match the situation.

Anxiety

It's **normal to worry** or be anxious sometimes. If you feel you are stuck worrying too much, **do something you enjoy** to take your mind off the topic.

Mood swings

Ever felt **happy** one minute and **angry** the next? This is known as a mood swing. These can be normal — especially during puberty, when hormones are working to help the body grow.

Talk it out

Sharing our feelings with others is important. **Chatting to someone** makes a problem **seem less scary**, and can help us think about a problem in a new way. Try talking to a trusted friend or family member.

SLEEPING WELL is important for mood. People can **FEEL CRANKY** if they don't get enough sleep.

Low mood
Feeling low sometimes is normal. **Exercising**, listening to **music**, or **playing** with a friend can help to lift your mood again.

Hormones
These **chemical messengers** from the brain affect our emotions. Dopamine (a **happy hormone**) makes us feel good. Adrenaline gets us ready to run fast!

Remember to refuel your body with food after exercising.

Get moving
Physical activity **pumps blood to the brain**, and hormones that make us feel good are released.

Have fun
What are your hobbies? Making **time** for **things you enjoy** will focus your attention in a positive way and help you **feel relaxed** and recharged.

199

Body talk

No matter what you look like, your body is a really **amazing** thing, and you should celebrate it!

I'm proud of my clean teeth!

Body image

"Body image" is how a person feels about their body. There might be times when a person wishes they looked different, and it can make them sad. **Comparing ourselves to others** can also affect how we see our own bodies. It can make us think we need to change ourselves to fit in.

Taking care of your body
The most important thing is to keep your body healthy with a varied diet, regular exercise, lots of sleep, and doing things that make you happy.

Be yourself
Sometimes the images we see on **television** or **social media** have been edited by computers. We shouldn't try to compare ourselves to the people we see in the media, because it's not always real!

Seeing clearly
Having a healthy body image means trying to accept and appreciate the wonderful things your body can do – such as cuddling a pet, or feeling the splash of ocean waves. Your body is an amazing natural tool that helps you experience the world!

It is important not to overeat or undereat if you don't like your size, because both can be bad for your health.

Let's celebrate!
What are some things you love about the way you look?

I like wearing my colourful glasses!

My freckles make lots of different patterns!

I love my hair!

Finding a balance
People are naturally **different sizes**, so even if you're bigger or smaller than your friends, it doesn't mean you're "too fat" or "too thin". Your doctor can tell you if you're a healthy weight.

Body bugs

The human body is home to trillions of **tiny lifeforms** that help to **keep us healthy**.

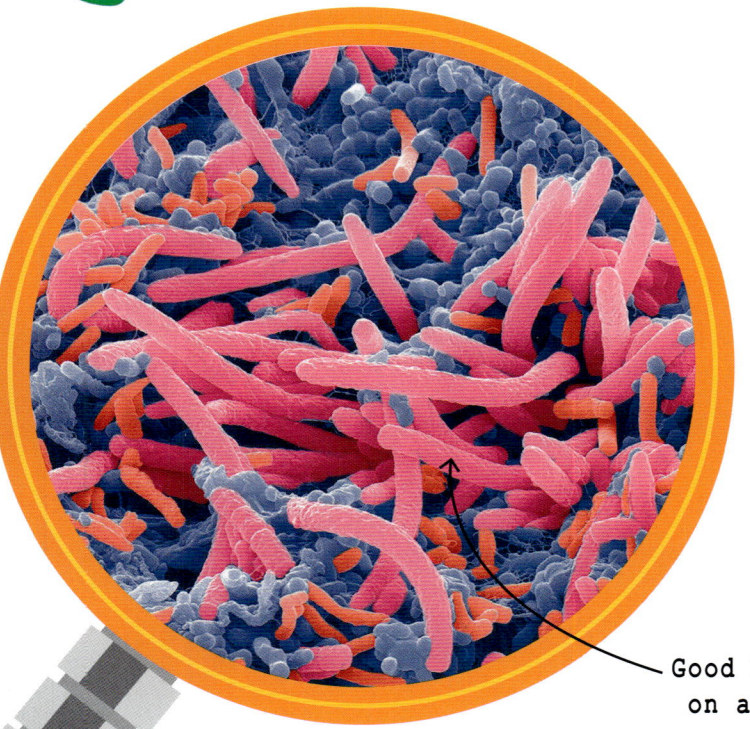

Tiny helpers
Microorganisms (or microbes) are tiny bugs too small to see. Bad bugs such as **germs** can make us itchy or ill, but many microbes **help** keep the body healthy.

Good bacteria on a tongue

Born this way
You get some of these **microorganisms** when you are born, so they are at work your **whole life**, keeping you going.

The microbe "Bdellovibrio" can move 600 times its body length per second. That makes it the fastest organism in the world!

Microbiome

Inside the **intestines** is a tiny world called the **microbiome**. The microorganisms that live here **protect** against diseases, help **digest** food, and make important **vitamins**. Eating a varied diet keeps the microbiome healthy.

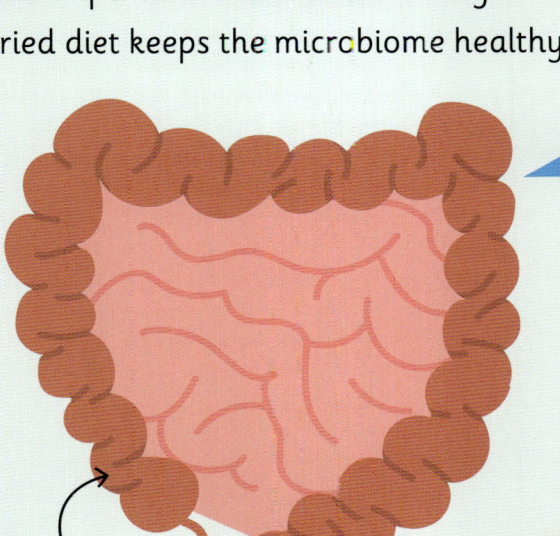

Intestines

Microbes may be tiny but they can survive in any environment – from inside the body to the bottom of the ocean.

There are lots of helpful microbes that live on the outside of the body as well. Some eat dead skin cells to keep us looking fresh, and others keep your eyelashes healthy.

Head chef

Bad bugs in our food can make us sick. But some **good bugs** actually help make **yummy foods** that people eat all the time. The way some microbes react with certain food and ingredients has given us things like **bread**, **yoghurt**, and **cheese**.

Battle it out
Pathogens are microscopic life forms that cause **disease**. These tiny troublemakers include bad bacteria, viruses, and fungi. The body has lots of ways to **protect itself** even from the smallest of villains!

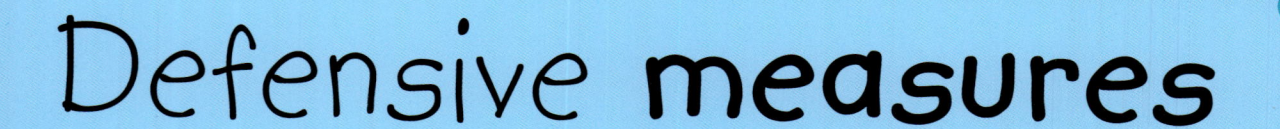

Defensive measures

Bad germs (known as pathogens) love warm and moist places, just like the human body. But the **immune system** is made up of cells and organs that **defend the body** from these tiny invaders.

Snot (mucus) traps dirt. It's really

Natural defences

Skin is the first line of defence, stopping pathogens from entering the body. Body **fluids** like tears and saliva have anti-bacterial properties. Stomach acid can kill any pathogen that enters it. A raised temperature also helps **kill germs** that are making you sick.

Army of defence cells

The body has lots of special defence cells that **protect** it in different ways. Some patrol the body, hunting down invaders. Others swallow pathogens! Others produce **antibodies** – proteins that can get rid of unwanted invaders.

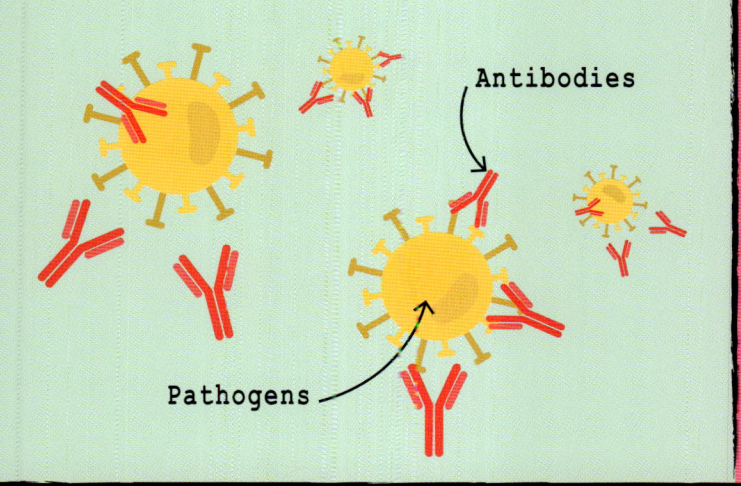

Antibodies

Pathogens

Helping hands

Like any **bodily systems**, sometimes the immune system doesn't work as it should. This can **affect the function** of many different organs. In such cases, the immune system needs a bit of **extra medical help**, such as medicines or physical therapy.

sticky, so PATHOGENS get stuck in it.

Staying safe

Here are some top tips to be prepared, **deal with an emergency**, and help keep everyone **safe at home**.

Healthy home

The adults in your home are responsible for keeping things **safe and tidy**. But here are some ways you can help to keep your home a safe and tidy place, too:

- Make sure the cords and cables from your devices are tucked away where people can't trip on them.

- Keep a clear pathway from your bed to the bedroom door so you don't trip in the night.

- Don't consume food or drink if it is past its expiry date, or you don't know where it came from.

- Clear up toys after playing with them. This is important if you have a baby or toddler in your home, as they might try to put small toys in their mouth.

- Don't leave glasses and plates too close to the edge of the table in case they fall and break.

- Don't run up or down the stairs, and hold the handrail if there is one.

Don't talk to strangers!
Tell a trusted adult if anyone says or does something that you're not comfortable with – whether online or in real life.

Never open a bottle, jar, or container without asking an adult first.

Dangerous situations
If you find yourself in a **dangerous situation**, follow the safety instructions you're given. Listen to a trusted adult to find out what to do, and follow **safety signs** and guidelines if there are any.

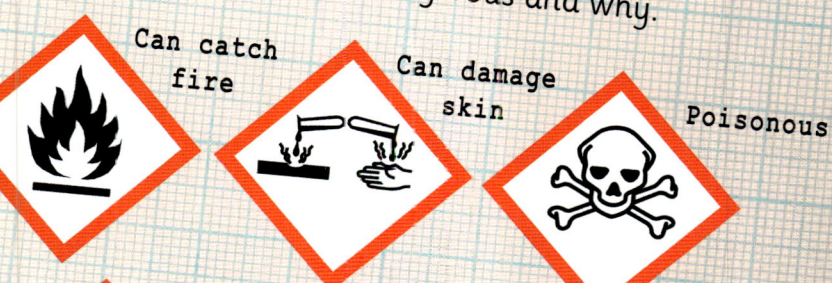

Traffic safety
Wait for the **pedestrian light** to go on, and look both ways before **crossing the street**. Don't run in or near the road. If you are carrying something, keep hold of it so you don't drop it in the road.

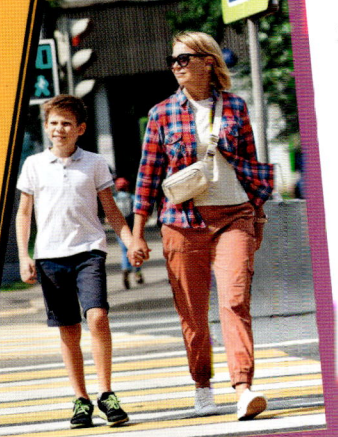

Danger zone
Cleaning products are all **full of chemicals** that can help keep things safe from bad germs. But these chemicals can be **harmful to the body** if you touch them directly. Labels with pictures are used to let people know what products are dangerous and why.

- Can catch fire
- Can damage skin
- Poisonous
- General warning
- Bad for the environment

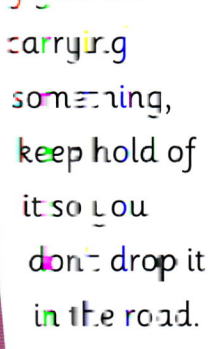

207

All kitted out

A **first aid kit** is a go-to tool for care and treatment of **minor accidents** and **injuries** at home. Let's find out what goes in a useful first aid kit.

For emergencies:

Contact numbers for emergency services, immediate family, and local doctors

For health and hygiene:

First Aid Manual

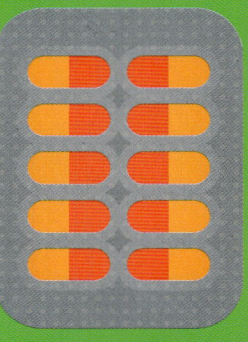

Painkillers (but aspirin is not suitable for people under 16)

Disposable gloves

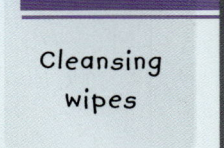

Cleansing wipes

It's a good idea to memorize your parent or guardian's mobile number, and to know your own address. This can be very useful in an emergency.

EMERGENCY! If there is a serious accident, the first aid kit won't be able to provide all the help a person needs. Instead, they may need to go to the hospital or call an ambulance by phoning 999.

For cuts and scrapes:

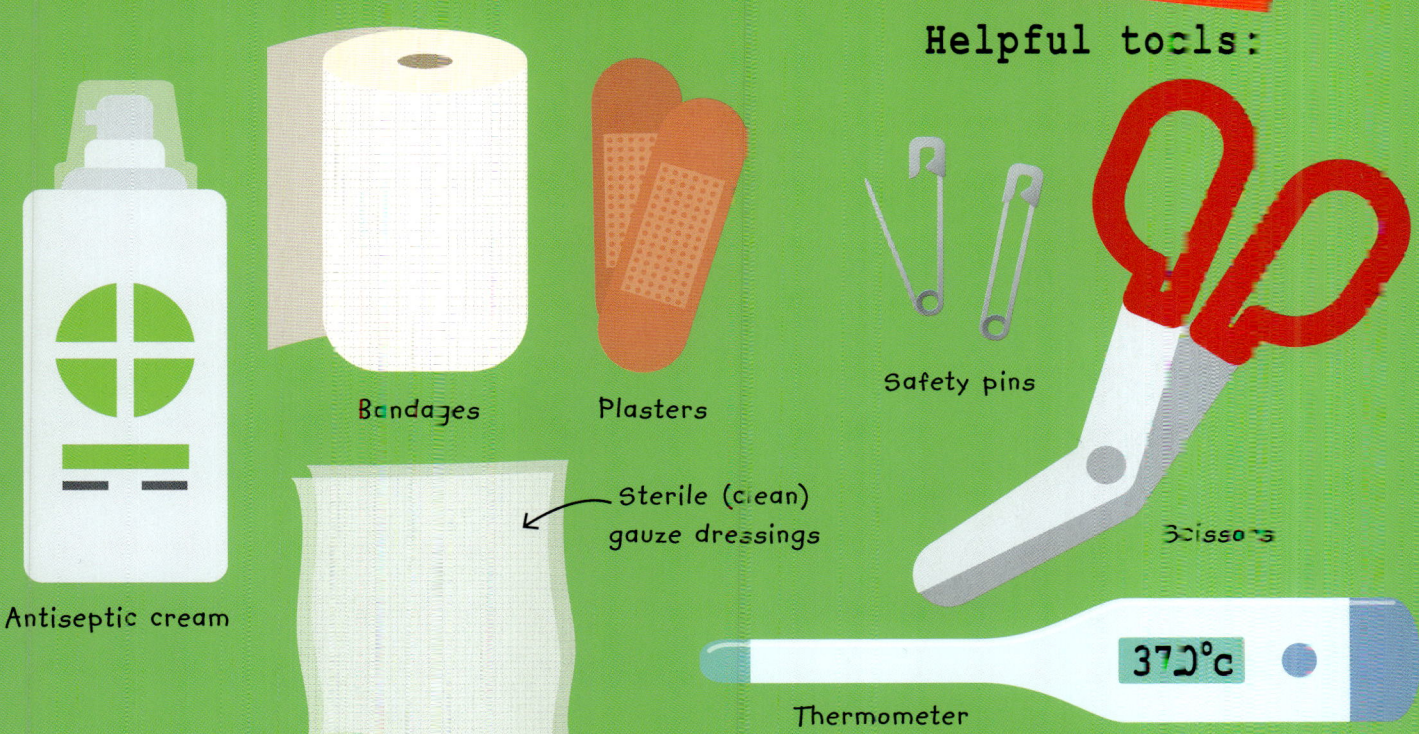

Antiseptic cream

Bandages

Plasters

Sterile (clean) gauze dressings

Helpful tools:

Safety pins

Scissors

Thermometer — 37.0°c

For sore skin and stings:

Cream or tablets for allergic reactions

For splinters:

Tweezers

Never take any medicine or tablets unless they are given to you by a trusted adult. Medicines can be dangerous when taken by the wrong person, or in the wrong way.

Finding THE FAKES

Groundbreaking news

Medicine can be dangerous, especially if it is fake. A group of girls in Africa came up with their own smart solution to find the fakes!

The members of Team Save-A-Soul are Promise Nnalue, Vivian Okoye, Adaeze Onuigbo, Jessica Osita, and Nwabuaku Ossai.

Fake

Fake goods
Medicine is a very important resource. Some criminals make fake, cheap medicine so they can sell it to make money.

Up for the challenge
The Technovation Challenge is a competition for girls aged 8–18. The goal is to fix problems using technology. Five girls in Nigeria decided to create an app to help protect people from accidentally buying dangerous, fake medicine.

App from scratch

The girls called themselves Team Save-A-Soul. They learnt how to build a mobile app from scratch. Their app, FD-Detector, reads the barcode on medicine to check if it is the real thing. If no authentic information is found, the medicine is thrown away.

Pain relief pills are the world's best-selling medicine.

Challenge champions

Their hard work paid off and Team Save-A-Soul became one of the winning teams of the Technovation Challenge in 2018! All of the team's members decided to go to university to keep learning and finding ways to make the world a better place.

Be careful

If you are unwell or in pain, never take any medicine or pain relief unless it is given to you by a trusted adult. Medicines can be safe for some people, but harmful to others.

At the dentist

Dentists know how to keep the **mouth** and **teeth** healthy. Sometimes, they can even tell if other parts of the body are healthy, just by looking in the mouth and at the teeth!

Brushing twice a day keeps the teeth healthy. It also makes the dentist's job easier!

Glasses
Wearing these glasses protects the dentist's eyes from any fluid that can splash while they are at work.

Open wide
Dentists check your teeth and mouth to make sure they are in good shape. They can tell you if you are **eating too much sugar** or not brushing your teeth properly. They can also treat problems such as **cavities** (holes in the teeth).

Suction
This machine makes a loud noise, but all it does is suck saliva out of your mouth so the dentist can see clearly.

Mouth mirror
This little mirror lets the dentist see around corners.

Bright light
The dentist might use a light to get a good view inside the mouth.

Gums and tongue
Dentists also check the health of the gums, tongue, and mouth. A tongue that is too smooth or too rough might mean the body is lacking important vitamins.

X-ray
An X-ray can show all your teeth – even the ones that have not come through yet.

Dental probe
This instrument is used to trace around every tooth so the dentist can tell if the teeth and gums are healthy.

Syringe
In some cases, the dentist might be able to give you anaesthetic with a syringe. Anaesthetic makes the mouth numb, so you can't feel anything while the dentist works on your teeth.

Check-up

If you don't feel well, then a check-up with your **doctor** is a good way to find out what's wrong. Health care workers use **special equipment** to check how the body is functioning and help them find a way to make you feel better.

Otoscope
This tool has a bright light that helps the doctor see the ear canal and the ear drum. They can tell if there's wax in the canal affecting hearing.

Say "ahhh"
Opening the mouth allows the doctor to look inside the mouth and throat. Saying "ahhh" lifts the roof of the mouth to make it easier for the doctor to see inside.

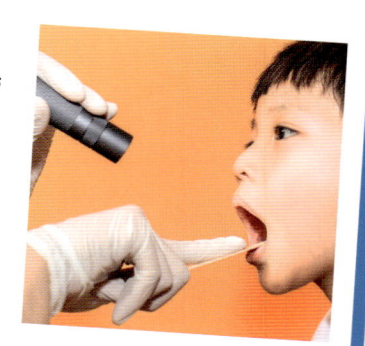

Stethoscope
This device is used to listen to the chest. Doctors can hear your heart and lungs working to check they are functioning well.

What a doctor does
Doctors make sure the body is healthy. If they think something isn't right, they are a bit like detectives. They work out what has **gone wrong** with the body and try to **put it right**.

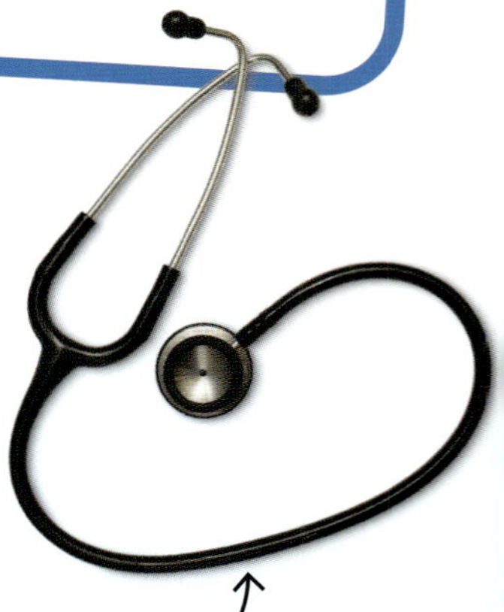

Stethoscope

Thermometer

A thermometer measures body temperature. It should be about 37 degrees Celsius (98.6 degrees Fahrenheit). There are different types of thermometers, such as digital, infrared scanner, and mercury thermometers.

Digital

Pulse

Taking a pulse means measuring how fast the heart beats every minute. To measure this, the doctor might place their fingers on your wrists, or use a machine. Pulses can be measured in many different places on the body.

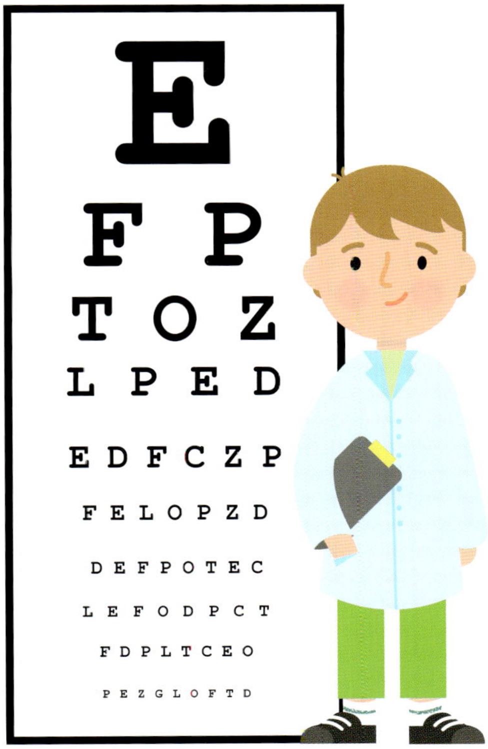

Vision

Reading letters of different sizes on a chart tests how well you can see. An optician (eye specialist) might also ask you to follow their moving finger with your eyes. This tests the eye muscles.

Stadiometer and scales

A stadiometer measures your height, and scales measure your weight. Measuring these things helps the doctor understand how your body is growing.

215

Space doctor

For many people, it's easy to go to a **doctor** for a check-up. But imagine you've **blasted off into space** and then develop a pain. You'd need to give Dr Serena Auñón-Chancellor a call!

Seeing stars
Dr Serena Auñón-Chancellor grew up in the US, dreaming of **becoming an astronaut**.

Phone home
Her first job was as a **doctor for the crew** of the International Space Station (ISS). Astronauts with health issues in space contacted Serena on Earth.

Out of this world

In 2018, Dr Auñón-Chancellor spent six months on board the ISS. She continued doing medical research and studies in space.

Feet on the ground

Back on Earth, Dr Auñón-Chancellor is involved with the Artemis program, an international space project to **build a station on the Moon**. She is also researching whether it is possible to **grow food** in space.

> I went to NASA Space Camp, which teaches young people useful science skills.

Doctor on call!

Some doctors work in very **extreme environments**, like these:

Submarines. There's often one doctor to handle hundreds of **patients on board**.

Antarctica. Doctors at research stations **help the scientists** there, and do medical research.

Ski resorts. Emergency doctors handle injuries on the steep, snowy ski slopes.

217

Human body words

This book is filled with words about the human body. Some can be a little tricky, so if you ever get stuck, look here.

Adapt When an animal or plant adapts, it changes over time to help it survive in its environment.

Adrenaline A hormone that is produced when a person is stressed or excited. It can make the body sweat and the heart beat faster.

Artery A tube that carries blood from the heart to the whole body.

Blood vessel A tube that carries blood around the body. Arteries and veins are types of blood vessels.

Cell The smallest structure in the human body, such as blood cells and bone cells.

Chemical A substance that cannot be broken down without changing it into something else, such as water or oxygen.

Diagnose To identify an illness. Doctors, scientists, and other medical workers use tests and examinations to diagnose a person's problem.

Diet The food that a person usually eats. A healthy diet contains plenty of fruit and vegetables.

DNA A chemical found in cells that carries instructions for how a human, animal, or plant develops. DNA stands for "deoxyribonucleic acid."

Gene A section of DNA that controls how a person or organism looks and grows.

Gland A group of cells that produce one or more substances. Glands do different jobs, such as producing sweat.

Gravity The force that pulls us down and keeps us on the ground. In space, there is only a tiny amount of gravity, which is why astronauts float.

Hormone A chemical messenger that travels around the bloodstream, affecting the way the body works.

Impaired If a person is impaired, it means they have a disability that causes something in the body to not work as well as it might.

Infection A disease, such as a cold or chickenpox, that is caused by germs.

Ligament Ligaments hold bones together. They are tough and strong pieces of tissue.

Melanin A substance that controls the colour of a person's skin and hair. The more melanin a person has, the darker their skin is.

Mucus A thick liquid that keeps the nose moist and helps to trap dirt.

Nerve A thread-like structure that sends and receives electrical messages between the brain and body.

Nutrient A substance that is found in food and helps animals and plants to grow.

Organ A part of the body that does a special job. Some of the main organs are the heart, brain, and lungs.

Platelet When someone is cut and bleeds, special blood cells called platelets help the blood to clot and help to seal the wound.

Prosthetic An artificial part of the body that is used as a replacement if a person is missing that part, such as a leg or a hand.

Pulse A pulse is the regular beat of blood going through the body. Pulses can be measured in different places, including the wrists.

Radio wave An invisible wave that sends signals through the air. Radio waves are used in MRI scans.

Receptor A nerve ending that senses changes in the body's environment, such as light or heat.

Reflex An action we do without thinking about it, such as blinking or sneezing.

Saliva A liquid that forms in the mouth to keep the mouth moist and make it easier to swallow.

Sensor A sensor reacts to input, such as light, heat, or smell, and sends the information to the brain.

Spinal cord The spinal cord carries messages between the brain and the rest of the body.

Tendon Tendons are rope-like tissues that join muscle to bone.

Tissue Cells that do the same job join together to form tissue.

Ultraviolet (UV) ray A ray of light from the sun that can damage the skin.

Vein A tube that carries blood from the whole body back to the heart.

Virus A tiny organism that can cause a disease.

Index

A
adolescence 28
adrenal glands 31
adrenaline 160, 161, 169, 199
adults 29
age 32–3
al-Razi, Abu Bakr 152, 153
allergies 168–71, 179
amputations 109
angiograms 13
animals 33, 34–5, 37, 43, 45, 47, 56–7, 61, 67, 71, 79, 85, 125, 126, 131, 133, 136–9, 141, 157, 168
antibiotics 157, 186
antibodies 205
anxiety 198
arms 62–3
arteries 105, 108, 109
asthma 101, 171

B
babies 12, 28, 35, 51, 61, 78–9, 80–1, 196
bacteria 165, 167, 186, 204
balance 34, 74, 123, 134–5, 149
bladder 67, 113, 119
blinking 61, 94
blood 20, 52, 104–5, 106–9, 113, 182, 194, 195
blood clots 184
blood pressure 31
blood transfusions 107
blood vessels 13, 82, 85, 108–9, 180–1, 182
body image 200–1
body language 93
body systems 11, 16–17, 21
bone marrow 50
bones 13, 15, 20, 24, 41, 43, 46–7, 50–1, 52, 56, 62–3, 64, 66, 68, 74, 184–5
Braille 141
brain 12, 13, 15, 16, 21, 34, 35, 39, 48, 49, 58, 77, 88–91, 126, 130, 139, 140–1, 142, 148, 148–9, 149
breathing 100–3, 171
bruises 180–1, 184

C
calcium 50
carbohydrates 193, 194
carbon 19
carbon dioxide 100, 102
cardiac muscle 54, 55
cardiovascular system 104–5
cartilage 45, 64, 136, 137
cells 20–1, 24, 25, 52, 106
children 28
choking 173
choroid 125
circulatory system 17, 108–9
collagen 50
colour-blindness 127
communication 35, 58, 92–3
compact bone 50
connective tissue 53
cornea 125
coughing 162, 164, 165, 172, 173
COVID-19 167
cranium 48, 49
crime scenes 24, 73
cuts and scrapes 182–3, 209

D
dairy produce 175, 193
decibels 132
dentists 212–13
dermis 82
dialysis 113
diaphragm 101
diet 32, 38, 46, 190–3, 200, 203
digestive system 17, 31, 97, 114–17
disabilities 26–7, 45, 63
diseases 164–7
DNA 21, 24–5, 81
doctors 214–17
dopamine 199
dreams 158–9
dyslexia 89

E
ears 48, 54, 122, 130–5, 214
EEG 12
emergencies 208, 209
emotions 91, 95, 160, 198
enamel 97
endocrine system 17, 30
endoskeletons 45
epidemics 167
epidermis 82
epithelium tissue 53
exercise 32, 194–5, 199, 200
exoskeletons 45
eyes 39, 99, 122, 124–9, 160, 215

F
face 49, 94–5
facial expressions 92, 93, 94–5
fat 193
feet 68, 74–5
femur 51, 62
fevers 156–7
fight, flight, freeze 160–1
fingerprints 72–3
fingers 68–9, 70
first aid kit 208–9
Fleming, Alexander 186
follicles 86
food 18, 30, 31, 36, 79, 114–17, 143–7, 169, 174, 175, 190–3, 194, 203
fractures 184–5
freckles 83
fruit and vegetables 192

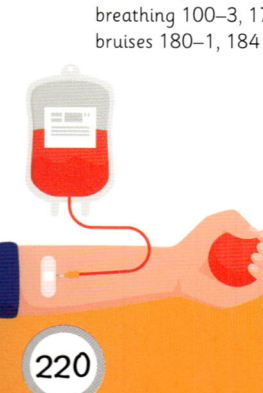

220

G
gas exchange 102
genes 21, 22–3, 25, 38, 46, 80, 87
germs 162, 164–5, 166, 169, 204–5
glands 30–1, 47, 75, 82, 98
gluteus maximus 55
gravity 37, 47
growth 28, 30, 46–7, 50

H
hair 22–3, 24, 38, 82, 86–7, 135, 136, 137, 154–5
hands 68–9, 123
hay fever 170–1
head lice 154–5
hearing 122, 130–5
heart 16, 21, 31, 104–5, 108–9, 160, 214, 215
height 46–7, 215
Hippocrates 152
home safety 206–7
hormones 30–1, 118, 160, 198, 199
hunger 123, 148, 190
hydrogen 18, 19

I
imagination 34, 90–1
immune system 17, 165, 169, 195, 204–5
infection 156–7, 182, 183
inheritance 21, 22, 46
insects 141, 169, 178–9
instincts 123, 160–1
integumentary system 16
interoception 148
intestines 31, 115, 116–17, 203
irises 124

J, K
Jenner, Edward 166
joints 15, 62, 64–5
jumping 56–7
keratin 71
kidneys 17, 112–13

L
language 35, 93
learning 89, 91
legs 62–3
lenses 125
life stages 28–9
lifespan 32–3
lifestyle 29, 32, 46, 47, 195
ligaments 48, 64
limbs 62–3
liver 112–13
lungs 16, 21, 101, 102, 103, 160, 172, 214
lymph nodes 110, 111
lymphatic system 17, 110–11

M
McClintock, Barbara 23
malaria 187
mandible 48
medicine 152–3, 169, 179, 186–7, 205, 209, 210–11
melanin 83
memory 91
meninges 49
mental health 198–9
metabolism 31
microbes 202–3
microbiome 203
microscopes 12
moles 83
moods 30, 198, 199
mouth 102, 212–13, 214
movement 41, 44, 50, 53, 54–5, 62–3
MRI 13
mucus 136, 137, 204–5
muscle tissue 52, 53
muscles 14, 18, 20, 38, 41, 56, 94, 194, 195
muscular system 16
musculoskeletal system 54
myelin sheaths 59

N
nails 70–1
nerves 58–9, 69
nervous system 16, 58–9, 149
nervous tissue 53
nitrogen 19
nose 102, 123, 136–7, 153
nutrients 78, 79, 104, 106, 113, 114–15, 116, 125, 194

O
oesophagus 115, 172, 175
old age 29
optical illusions 128–9
organ transplants 113
organs 15, 16, 21, 44, 52, 67
osteons 50
osteoporosis 184
oxygen 18, 19, 31, 37, 73, 100–1, 102, 104–5, 108, 194

P
pacemakers 105
pain 88, 141, 174–5, 182, 211
pancreas 31
pandemics 167
pathogens 204–5
pelvis 66–7
penicillin 186
pineal gland 31
pituitary gland 31
placenta 78
plaque 97
plasma 107
platelets 107, 183
pollen 170–1
poo 66, 115, 117
pores 98
prefrontal cortex 90
pregnancy 66, 78–9, 80
proprioception 149
prosthetic body parts 45, 57, 63, 67
proteins 192, 194, 205
pupils 124, 160

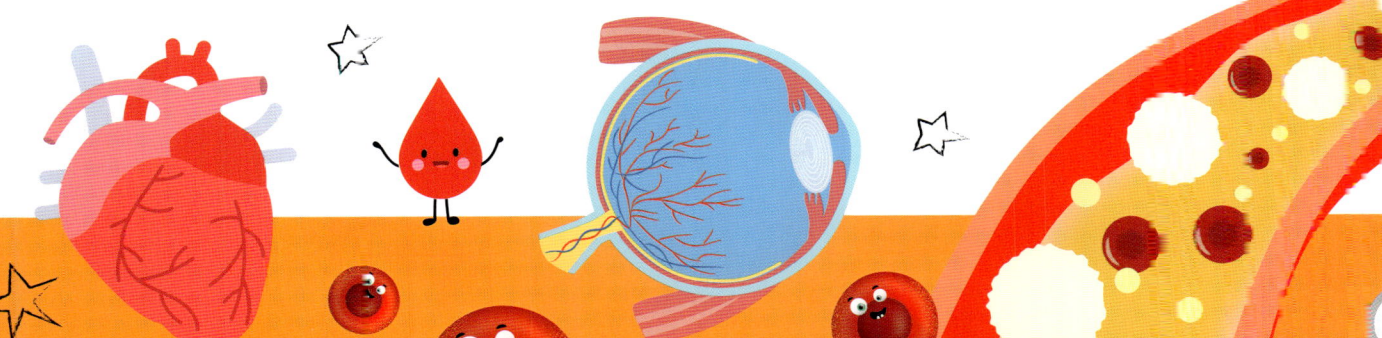

221

R

receptors 60, 61, 139, 140, 182
rectum 117
reflexes 60–1
reproductive system 17, 67
respiratory system 17, 100–3
retinas 125
Röntgen, Wilhelm 42–3
roots (hair) 82, 86
roots (nails) 70
roots (teeth) 97

S

saliva 99, 115, 175, 205
scars 183
sclera 125
senses 34–5, 120–49
sick, feeling/being 174–5
sign language 92
skeletal muscle 54, 55
skeletal system 16
skeleton 41, 44–5
skin 14, 52, 75, 82–3, 176–7, 180–3
skull 48–9
sleep 31, 32, 36, 37, 158–9, 196–7, 200
sleepwalking 159
smell 93, 122, 123, 136–9, 146, 147
smooth muscle 54, 55
sneezing 60, 61, 162–3, 164, 165, 170, 171
speech 93
spinal cord 58, 60
spine 46, 51
spongy bone 50, 184
stings 169, 178–9, 209
stoma 117
stomach 31, 115, 172, 174–5, 190–1
strangers 207
sun safety 176–7
swallowing 172–3
sweat 75, 82, 85, 98, 161
synaesthesia 148

T

taste 122, 123, 142–7
taste buds 142, 143, 145
tears 98, 99, 205
teeth 13, 24, 43, 96–7, 212–13
temperature 83, 84–5, 86, 156–7, 205, 215
tendons 64, 65, 68
thoughts 90
throat 172–3, 214
thumbs 34, 68
thyroid gland 31
tissues 20–1, 52–3
toes 70, 74
tongue 123, 213
touch 70, 122, 123, 140–1, 146
traffic safety 207
twins 25, 80–1

U, V

ulnar nerve (funny bone) 51
ultrasound 12, 79
umbilical cord 78
urethra 113
urinary system 17, 119
vaccines 166–7
veins 105, 108, 109
viruses 39, 156, 165, 167, 173, 174, 204
vision 39, 122, 124–9, 141, 146, 215

W, X, Y

waste 112–17, 119
water 18–19, 36, 118–19
wee 66, 113, 119
weight 201, 215
wheelchairs 27, 63
windpipe 172, 173
winking 94
womb 66, 78
X-rays 13, 42–3, 213
Youyou, Tu 186, 187

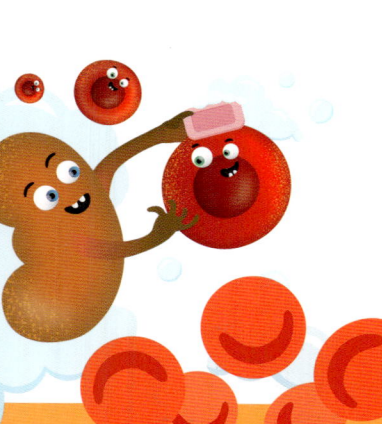

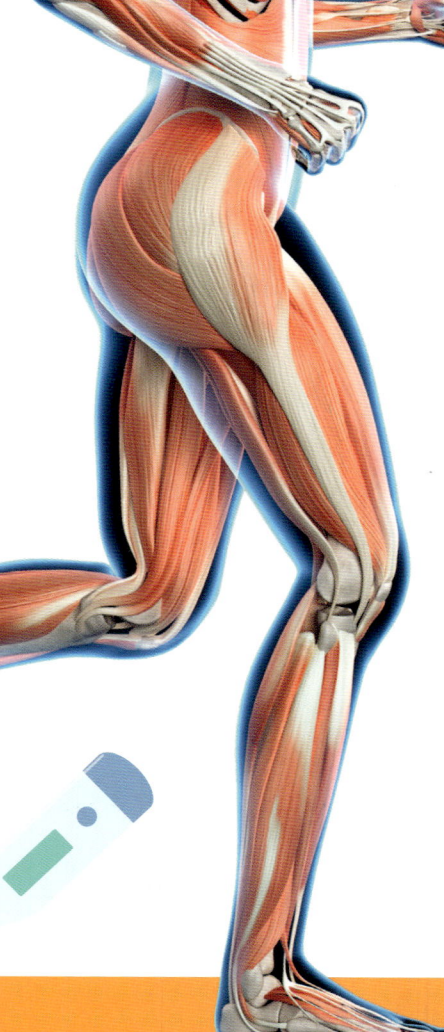

Acknowledgements

DK would like to thank: Francesco Piscitelli for proofreading, Helen Peters for compiling the index, Vagisha Pushp and Rituraj Singh for picture research, Sif Nørskov and Eleanor Bates for design assistance, and Abi Luscombe, Abi Maxwell, and Sophie Parkes for editorial assistance.

The publisher would like to thank the following for their kind permission to reproduce their photographs:

(Key: a-above; b-below/bottom; c-centre; f-far; l-left; r-right; t-top)

1 123RF.com: Dndavis (tr/handprint); Volodimir Kalina (bl). **3 Dreamstime.com:** Erikreis (b). **Getty Images:** Westend61 (clb). **5 123RF.com:** alexzaitsev (br). **Dreamstime.com:** Jimmyi23 (tl); Xsviatx (br/Brain). **6-7 123RF.com:** alexzaitsev (b). **6 Dreamstime.com:** Elena Schweitzer / Egal (br). **Getty Images:** Stone / Catherine Delahaye (bc). **7 Dreamstime.com:** Davidebner (b). **8 Dreamstime.com:** Olga Nalynskaya (x3); Waroot Tangtumsatid (bl); Nataliia Prokofyeva / Valiza14 (br). **9 Dreamstime.com:** Elena Schweitzer / Egal (br). **10-11 123RF.com:** alexzaitsev (b). **Dreamstime.com:** Zoom-zoom (t). **11 123RF.com:** Brian Kinney (tl). **Dreamstime.com:** Fizkes (b). **12 123RF.com:** Zoia Fedorova (c). **Dreamstime.com:** Elena Schweitzer / Egal (cl); Sofiia Shunkina (tr); Vienybe (cr). **13 Alamy Stock Photo:** Samunella (tr). **Dreamstime.com:** Itsmejust (tc). **Shutterstock.com:** PROFFIPhoto (bl). **15 Dreamstime.com:** Famveldman (cra). **18 123RF.com:** Juri Samsonov (cr). **18-19 Dreamstime.com:** Oleksiy (b). **19 Dreamstime.com:** Alexyndr (cra). **20 Dreamstime.com:** Puntasit Choksawatdikorn (crb). **21 Getty Images:** Science Photo Library / Steve Gschmeissner (cr). **Shutterstock.com:** nobeastsofierce (bl). **22-23 Dreamstime.com:** Stephen Denness (c), Rzoze19 (t). **23 Dreamstime.com:** Andrii Bezvershenko (b/x6); THPStock (tr). **Science Photo Library:** Smithsonian Institution (cr). **24 123RF.com:** drmicrobe (bl). **Dreamstime.com:** Makovskyi Artem (bl/red hair); Olga Nalynskaya (tr/x2). **25 Dreamstime.com:** Alptraum (tl); Vasyl Helevachuk (tc); Ryan Simpson (tr); Alena Brozova (tr/leaf); Axel Bueckert (cla); Hudakore (crc); Isselee (clb); Todd Taulman (crb); Waroot Tangtumsatid (br). **Science Photo Library:** TEK IMAGE (cb). **26 Dreamstime.com:** Helder Almeida (bc). **27 Getty Images / iStock:** E+ / momcilog (crb). **28 123RF.com:** jovannig (clb). **Dreamstime.com:** Anna Demidova, Veronika Seppanen (clb/baby); Eric Simard (cr); Studioloco (cr). **29 Alamy Stock Photo:** REUTERS / Bobby Yip (c). **Dreamstime.com:** Funkeyfactory (cl). **Getty Images:** Moment / Image taken by Mayte Torres (c); Tetra images / Shestock (cr). **30 Dreamstime.com:** Nagy-bagoly Ilona (t). **32 123RF.com:** Gino Santa Maria (cl). **Dreamstime.com:** Microvone (br); Rommeo79 (ca); Jesada Wongsa (c). **33 Dreamstime.com:** Cienpies Design / Illustrations (cb); Stubblefieldphoto (b); Natchapohn (tc); Anna Suchkova (tl); Planetfelicity (ca); Isselee (cr); Veniamin Kraskov (br); Igor Zakharevich (cr). **Getty Images:** Pascal Parrot / Sygma (c). **34 Dreamstime.com:** Design56 (bc); Classic Vector (c); Kengmerry (bc/cloud); Rina Puspitaningrum (cr); Nataliia Prokofyeva / Valiza14 (br). **35 Alamy Stock Photo:** ZSSD / Minden Pictures (crb). **Dreamstime.com:** Kengmerry (bl); Tom Wang (tr). **Getty Images:** 500px / Matthias Gudath (cla). **36 Dreamstime.com:** Igoriss (b); Nop2000 (cl). **Shutterstock.com:** ANL (cb). **36-37 Getty Images / iStock:** E+ / hometowncd. **37 Dreamstime.com:** THPStock (bl/Paper); Vadim Yerofeyev (cla); Zoryen (tr/Graph). **Getty Images:** Paul Foster / EyeEm (tc); The Chronicle Collection / Don Cravens (b). **Reuters:** STRINGER. (t). **Science Photo Library:** Power And Syred (crb). **Shutterstock.com:** Zuma (b). **38 Dreamstime.com:** Bigmouse108 (cr); Michael Flippo (clb); Hughstoneian (bc). **Getty Images:** Moment / Daniela Solomon (bc/boy's head). **39 Dreamstime.com:** Ozgur Coskun (tc); Xsviatx (c); Yusuf Demirci (bc); Flynt (br). **40 123RF.com:** Dndavis (br). **Dreamstime.com:** Sebastian Kaulitzki (crb, c); Valentyn75 (t). **41 Dreamstime.com:** Brendan Delany (bl); Sam74100 (tr). **42 Dreamstime.com:** Monthian Ritchan-ad / Thailoei92 (tr). **43 Alamy Stock Photo:** blickwinkel / F. Teigler (crb). **Dreamstime.com:** Borzywoj (cl). **45 123RF.com:** Tim Hester / timnester (c). **Alamy Stock Photo:** EThamPhoto / Erik Tham (cr); Jeff Gilbert (br). **Dreamstime.com:** Isselee (bl/Giraffe); Yobro10 (bl/Elephant); Pzaxe (c/Ladybird). **46 123RF.com:** tomwang (tl). **Dreamstime.com:** Golfxx (br); Lightkeeper (bl). **47 Alamy Stock Photo:** Vintage_Space (cr). **Dreamstime.com:** Anankkml (r). **48 Dreamstime.com:** Hughstoneian (b). **48-49 Dreamstime.com:** Valentyn75.

50 Dreamstime.com: 7active Studio (c); Tetiana Pavliuchenko (cra). **Getty Images / iStock:** E+ / SDI Productions (br). **51 Dreamstime.com:** Sebastian Kaulitzki / Mast3r (tc/x2); Oleksandr Malysh (tr). **52 Dreamstime.com:** Designstock (bl); Esriaxx (bc); Hongqi Zhang (aka Michael Zhang) (br). **53 Dreamstime.com:** Sara Paulicevic (c); Sam74100 (tl); Ruslan Shugushev (bl); Khosrork (br). **54 Dreamstime.com:** Tetiana Pavliuchenko (br). **54-55 Dreamstime.com:** Sebastian Kaulitzki (t). **55 Dreamstime.com:** Monkey Business Images (bl). **56 123RF.com:** lopolo (cr). **57 Alamy Stock Photo:** Aflo Co. Ltd. / Nippon News / SportsPressJP (t); REUTERS / Jerry Lampen (cr); Jim Cumming (br). **Dreamstime.com:** Neirfy (clb). **59 123RF.com:** Falcon Kitpaiboolwat (tr). **Dreamstime.com:** Famveldman (tl). **61 Dreamstime.com:** Toian Dixon (cra); Ramirezom (b). **Fotolia:** StarJumper (bc). **Getty Images / iStock:** E+ / gokhanilgaz (c). **62 Getty Images / iStock:** SolStock (br). **63 123RF.com:** Loreya Medina (b). **Getty Images:** Stone / Alistair Berg (cl). **64 123RF.com:** Roman Samotoskiy (b). **65 123RF.com:** Patrick Foto / pat138241 (c). **Getty Images / iStock:** Picsfive (cb). **66 Dreamstime.com:** Sebastian Kaulitzki (br); Dmytro Konstantynov (bl). **67 123RF.com:** Sebastian Kaulitzki (crb). **Dreamstime.com:** Sebastian Kaulitzki (cra); Tetiana Pavliuchenko (tl); Anastasia Tsoupa (br). **Shutterstock.com:** topimages (cb). **68 Dreamstime.com:** Aleksei Veprev (ca). **69 Dreamstime.com:** Evgeniia Parkhomenko (cra); Prostockstudio (bl); Anna Tolipova (tc); Tonitt (cr); Ultraonn (br). **70 Getty Images / iStock:** E+ / avid_creative (tl). **71 Dreamstime.com:** Feverpitched (cra); Isselee (bl); Kwanchaichaiudom (tl); Tlstarri (tr); Oleksandr Grybanov (br). **72 123RF.com:** Dndavis (c). **Dreamstime.com:** Artem Khabeev / Khabeev (fbr); German Ariel Berra (berra) (berra inc.) (br). **73 123RF.com:** Dndavis (cb). **Dreamstime.com:** Kevin Chesson (tr); Artem Khabeev / Khabeev (br). **74 Dreamstime.com:** Wavebreakmedia Ltd (b). **74-75 Dreamstime.com:** Brendan Delany (t). **75 Dreamstime.com:** Gajus (b); Kwanchaichaiudom (c); Wayada Sesa (c). **76 Dreamstime.com:** Yarruta (br). **78 Dreamstime.com:** Monkey Business Images (tl). **79 Depositphotos Inc:** NewAfrica (crb). **Dreamstime.com:** Paul Joyce (clb); Monkey Business Images (tr). **80 Dreamstime.com:** Felix Mizioznikov (cl). **Getty Images / iStock:** BorupFoto (b). **80-81 Dreamstime.com:** Zoom-zoom (t). **82-83 Dreamstime.com:** Tuk69tuk (t). **82 Dreamstime.com:** Famveldman (br); Vchalup (c). **83 Dreamstime.com:** Gunold (tr); Stefan Hermans (cb); Yulia (c). **84 Dreamstime.com:** Designua (bc). **Shutterstock.com:** Arite van den Broek (t). **85 123RF.com:** Vclav ebek (cra); viewstock (b). **Depositphotos Inc:** yanlev (tc). **Dreamstime.com:** Geoffrey Sperring (br). **86 123RF.com:** Dmitry Ageev (tr). **Dreamstime.com:** Fernandes Borges Michel (tr). **87 Dreamstime.com:** ammaspot (tl); Mario Ondris (c); Phana Sitti (tr). **88-89 Dorling Kindersley:** Egle Kazdailyte (Space). **90-91 Dreamstime.com:** Yarruta (Star and rocket). **90 Dreamstime.com:** Yarruta (br). **Getty Images:** OJO Images / Wealan Pollard (clb). **91 Dreamstime.com:** Yarruta (cr, br). **92 Dreamstime.com:** Warangkana Charuyodhin (c); Chernetskaya (t). **93 123RF.com:** Hung Chung Chih (bl). **Dreamstime.com:** Godfer (cra); Kobyakov (tr); Kwanchaichaiudom (br). **94 Getty Images / iStock:** E+ / CarlFourie (t). **95 123RF.com:** Karel Joseph Noppe Brooks (clb). **Dreamstime.com:** Lightfieldstudiosprod (br); Sherrie Smith (c). **Getty Images / iStock:** E+ / stock_colors (tl). **Getty Images:** Moment / Jesus Calonge (t). **96 Dreamstime.com:** Julie Burmistrova (crb); Barbara Helgason (cb); Iadamson (t). **97 Depositphotos Inc:** taonga (crb). **Dreamstime.com:** Keithspaulding (tr). **98 Dreamstime.com:** Aperturesound (b). **98-99 Dreamstime.com:** Pop Nukoonrat (t). **99 Dreamstime.com:** Yulia Ryabokon (cb); Marian Vejcik (tr). **Getty Images / iStock:** E+ / longyuan (bl); Sudowoodo (tc); praetorianphoto (br). **100 123RF.com:** Maksym Bondarchuk (tr). **Dreamstime.com:** Iryna1 (c/Forest). **100-101 Dreamstime.com:** Zuzana Tillerova (b). **101 Dreamstime.com:** Goce Risteski (br). **102 Dreamstime.com:** Alexandr Mitiuc (bc). **103 123RF.com:** mihtiander (c). **Dreamstime.com:** Chernetskaya (bl); Khosrork (ca). **Getty Images / iStock:** E+ / sturti (tl); E+ / simonkr (cr). **104 123RF.com:** skiny25 (cb). **Dreamstime.com:** Yobro10 (tl). **105 123RF.com:** Photowa (br); chaicheevinlikit (tr). **106 Dreamstime.com:** Flynt (clb). **107 Dreamstime.com:** Andrii Bezvershenko (cra); Izanbar (t). **111 Getty Images / iStock:** Jatinder Arora (br). **113 123RF.com:** Santiago Nunez Iniguez (tr). **Dreamstime.com:** Picsfve (br). **114 123RF.com:** Maksym Narodenko (tr). **Science Photo Library:** Lewis Houghton (crb). **117 Dreamstime.com:** Martina Hanakova (crb). **118 Dreamstime.com:**

223

Andreykuzmin (tl). **Fotolia:** Juri Samsonov (b). **119 123RF.com:** Kirill Kirsanov (crb). **Dreamstime.com:** Gaby Kooijman / Gabees (bl). **Fotolia:** Juri Samsonov (ca). **120 123RF.com:** Volodimir Kalina. **120-121 123RF.com:** alexzaitsev (b); neyro2008 (c). **121 Depositphotos Inc:** Lebval (t). **122 Dreamstime.com:** Ampack (clb). **Shutterstock.com:** Ollyy (br). **123 123RF.com:** Jacek Chabraszewski (br). **Dreamstime.com:** Siarhei Shuntsikau (tr). **Shutterstock.com:** Tverdokhlib (bc). **124 123RF.com:** Volodimir Kalina. **125 Dreamstime.com:** Michael Elliott (bc); Kazoka (br); Sofiia Potanina (cb); Paul Murphy (fbr). **127 123RF.com:** fotana (cla); Yuliia Sonsedska (bl). **Dreamstime.com:** Eveleen007 (cr). **128 Dreamstime.com:** Yurii Perepadia (r/x3). **129 Alamy Stock Photo:** Ray Evans (crb). **Dreamstime.com:** Tosca Weijers (clb); Andrius Zigmantas (tr). **131 Dreamstime.com:** Isselee (crb); Rudmer Zwerver (cra); Yairleibovich (br). **Getty Images:** Anna Averianova / 500px (c); Science & Society Picture Library (clb). **Science Photo Library:** PEAKSTOCK (tr). **133 Alamy Stock Photo:** REUTERS / Mike Blake (cra). **Depositphotos Inc:** niknikpo (bl). **134-135 Dreamstime.com:** Pop Nukoonrat (b). **134 Getty Images:** Stone / Catherine Delahaye (r). **135 123RF.com:** whitecity (t). **Dreamstime.com:** Iulius Costache (cb); Vladlislav Zhukov (ca). **136 Shutterstock.com:** Agnieszka Bacal (br). **137 Dreamstime.com:** Donyanedomam (bl). **Shutterstock.com:** bekirevren (br). **138 123RF.com:** neyro2008 (cl). **Dreamstime.com:** Carol Buchanan (bl). **139 123RF.com:** neyro2008 (tr). **Dreamstime.com:** Mchudo (clb). **140 Dreamstime.com:** Tashka2000 (br). **140-141 123RF.com:** alexzaitsev (b). **141 Dreamstime.com:** Pimmimemom (bc); Wave Break Media Ltd (tl); Anatoliy Samara (cr). **142 Depositphotos Inc:** Lebval (br). **143 Dreamstime.com:** Yarruta (tr). **144 Dreamstime.com:** Ruth Black (bc); Viktarm (br). **Getty Images:** Photodisc / Zing Images (tr). **145 Dreamstime.com:** Roberto Giovannini (tr, cra); Yalcinsonat (cra/Crisps). **146 Dreamstime.com:** Silas Brown (cl). **146-147 Dreamstime.com:** Ruslan Pantyushin (t). **147 Dreamstime.com:** Robyn Mackenzie (cla); Alexander Traksel (br). **148 123RF.com:** mahirates (cl); Wavebreak Media Ltd (br). **Dreamstime.com:** Aaron Amat (b). **150 Shutterstock.com:** Protasov AN (cla). **150-151 Dreamstime.com:** Sasinparaksa (b); Zoom-zoom (cla/sky). **Getty Images:** Westend61 (ca). **151 Shutterstock.com:** Raeldg (tr). **152 Alamy Stock Photo:** Artokoloro / Penta Springs (cl). **Dreamstime.com:** Michalbe (cra); Pop Nukoonrat (cra); Migfoto (bc). **153 Alamy Stock Photo:** Science History Images / Photo Researchers (bl); World History Archive (tr). **Dreamstime.com:** Alexey Koshelev (br/x3). **154 Dreamstime.com:** Jean Paul Chassenet (b); Lorna (crb/Blond hair). **Shutterstock.com:** Protasov AN (clb). **155 Dreamstime.com:** Aoo3771 (tr); Kwanchaichaiudom (clb/black hair); Hongqi Zhang (aka Michael Zhang) (b); Zts (br/Comb). **156 Dreamstime.com:** Yuri Arcurs (cl). **157 Dreamstime.com:** Tjkphotography (br). **Getty Images / iStock:** Ihor Kashurin (tl). **158-159 Dreamstime.com:** Sasinparaksa (b); Zoom-zoom (t/sky). **Getty Images:** Westend61 (t). **159 Dreamstime.com:** Poutnik (clb). **Getty Images / iStock:** E+ / bojanstory (ca). **160 Dreamstime.com:** Macrovector (cb); Classic Vector (clb). **160-161 Getty Images / iStock:** E+ / FatCamera. **161 Dreamstime.com:** Germanskydiver (tr). **162 Dreamstime.com:** Mcech (cb). **163 Dreamstime.com:** Kankhem (tl, tl/blackboard); Prostockstudio (bl). **164 Dreamstime.com:** Lightfieldstudiosprod (br). **165 Dreamstime.com:** Golfxx (cr); Greenland (tl). **166 Alamy Stock Photo:** Heike Riemer / Sddeutsche Zeitung Photo (b). **Dreamstime.com:** Georgios Kollidas (crb); Tawatchai Prakobkit (cl). **167 Alamy Stock Photo:** Pictorial Press Ltd (cra). **Dreamstime.com:** Luvvstudio (ca); Satori13 (clb); Fang Zheng (br). **168 Dreamstime.com:** Denys Prokofyev (c). **Getty Images:** Moment / seksan Mongkhonkhamsao (r). **168-169 Dreamstime.com:** Dgilder (b). **169 Dreamstime.com:** Aoldman (cra); Leonardo255 (tr); Pavel Naumov (clb); Worldofvector (cb); Furo_felix (bl); David Seymour (br). **170-171 Dreamstime.com:** Rodicabruma (b). **170 Alamy Stock Photo:** Dex Image (br). **Getty Images:** Martin McHale / 500px (/clb). **171 Dreamstime.com:** Chris Dorney (bc); Parinyabinsuk (tr); Wisconsinart (cr). **Getty Images:** DigitalVision / Taiyou Nomachi (tl). **172 Dreamstime.com:** Matthew Benoit (c); Tartilastock (tr/x10Pipes); Dmytro Zinkevych (tr/Girl); Prostockstudio (cb); Keerati (cb). **173 Dreamstime.com:** Makidotvn (tr); THPStock (tl). **174-175 Dreamstime.com:** Pop Nukoonrat (Background). **174 123RF.com:** tidty (tr). **Dreamstime.com:** Adolfolazo (clb). **Getty Images / iStock:** malerapaso (bl). **175 Alamy Stock Photo:** PA Images / Ben Curtis (clb). **Dreamstime.com:** Soumen Hazra (tl); Pojoslaw (cla); Kwanchaichaiudom (cra, br). **176-177 123RF.com:** Iakov Kalinin (t/Sky). **Dreamstime.com:** Viktor Gladkov (t). **176 Shutterstock.com:** Amelia Fox (bl). **177 123RF.com:** lynxtime (tl). **178-179 Shutterstock.com:** Dernkadel (t). **178 Depositphotos Inc:** Ale-ks (tr). **Dreamstime.com:** Jimmyi23 (cb); Verastuchelova (cr). **179 Depositphotos Inc:** Ale-ks (t/x4). **180 Alamy Stock Photo:** Ian Leonard (cr); Natalia Lukiianova (cb). **Dreamstime.com:** Lzf (br). **Shutterstock.com:** Raeldg (tr). **181 Shutterstock.com:** kornnphoto (br). **182 Dreamstime.com:** Mohamed Osama (br); Andrii Zorii (bl).

183 Dreamstime.com: Pichai Choosenpom (bl); Brendan Delany (tl); Phawat Khommai (cl). **184 Alamy Stock Photo:** Nucleus Medical Media Inc (bl). **Depositphotos Inc:** Crevis (tr). **Dorling Kindersley:** Arran Lewis (br). **185 Alamy Stock Photo:** Scott Camazine (br). **Getty Images / iStock:** Natalia Serdyuk (ca). **Shutterstock.com:** Yok_onepiece (bl). **186-187 Dreamstime.com:** Ana Sousa / Anadesousa. **186 Dreamstime.com:** Aviag7 (cr/Mold); Kateryna Kon (cl). **187 Dreamstime.com:** Mr.smith Chetanachan / Smuaya (tr). **188 Dreamstime.com:** Bulychevaart (tl); Nevinates (bl/Blueberries); Leszek Ogrodnik / Lehu (bl/Apple); Katerina Kovaleva (cr); Wavebreakmedia Ltd (br). **189 123RF.com:** ocusfocus (bl). **Dreamstime.com:** Tracy Decourcy / Rimglow (cla). **Getty Images / iStock:** Coprid (cb). **190-191 Dreamstime.com:** Serg_veluscesc (ca). **191 Shutterstock.com:** N.Savranska (cl). **192 123RF.com:** Reinis Bigacs (crb/beef). **Dorling Kindersley:** Geoff Brightling / South of England Rare Breeds Centre, Ashford, Kent (br/Eggs). **Dreamstime.com:** Katerina Kovaleva (ca); Tomboy2290 (tr/Lettuce); Tracy Decourcy / Rimglow (cra); Nevinates (cb/Blueberries); Leszek Ogrodnik / Lehu (cb/Apple). **Getty Images / iStock:** clintscholz (crb/Sardines). **193 Dreamstime.com:** Yuri Arcurs (cra); Etiennevoss (clb/mozzarella); Tatiana Muslimova (clb/Cheese); Svetlana Kuznetsova (clb/Butter). **Getty Images / iStock:** Coprid (clb/Milk). **194 Alamy Stock Photo:** Derek Meijer (cla). **Dreamstime.com:** Ryzhov Sergey (bl). **195 123RF.com:** ocusfocus (br). **Getty Images / iStock:** E+ / FatCamera (cl). **196 123RF.com:** Denis Tabler (r/Baby). **Dreamstime.com:** Ingridneumann (r). **197 Dreamstime.com:** Yanisa Deeratanasrikul (bl); Andrey Moisseyev (cla); Oksun70 (br). **Photolibrary:** White / Digital Zoo (cra). **198 Dreamstime.com:** Embe2006 (cra/x3); Fizkes (tr); Yobro10 (bc). **199 Dreamstime.com:** Kenishirotie (tr); Lightfieldstudiosprod (tl); Warrengoldswain (c); Natalia Sevriukova (bc). **Getty Images / iStock:** E+ / SDI Productions (br). **200 Dreamstime.com:** Erikreis (b). **201 Dreamstime.com:** Axstokes (tl); Lightfieldstudiosprod (tr); Stuartbur (b). **Getty Images:** Photographer's Choice RF / Jon Boyes (cl/plate). **202 Alamy Stock Photo:** Steve Gschmeissner / Science Photo Library (cl). **Dreamstime.com:** Bulychevaart (tl/bx2); Prostockstudio (crb). **203 Dreamstime.com:** Evgeny Karandaev / Karandaev (clb); Moneti (tr); Szefei (br). **204 Dreamstime.com:** Pipa100 (tl). **205 Dreamstime.com:** Olesia Bilkei (br). **206-207 Dreamstime.com:** Pop Nukoonrat (sky). **206 Dreamstime.com:** Kelttt; Kianlin (clb/Phone); Sergey Siz`kov (b/Train); Remus Rigo (clb). **207 Dreamstime.com:** Gmm2000 (bl); Julesunlimited (bl/x5); Vadim Yerofeyev (bl/Graph); Pockygallery11 (cra); Ryzhov Sergey (br). **Getty Images:** Eskay Lim / EyeEm (ca). **208 123RF.com:** jemastock (cl). **209 Dreamstime.com:** Yuri Arcurs (br). **210-211 Getty Images / iStock:** Zocha_K. **211 123RF.com:** anthonycz (br); Janek Sergejev (cr). **Dreamstime.com:** Yuri Arcurs (tl). **Getty Images / iStock:** E+ / sanjeri (cl). **212-213 Dreamstime.com:** Wavebreakmedia Ltd. **212 Dreamstime.com:** Svetlana Akifyeva (cl). **213 Alamy Stock Photo:** Marko Rupena (tc). **Dreamstime.com:** Andrejsv (cr). **214 Dreamstime.com:** Elnur (tr); Wanuttapong Suwannasilp (cra); Robert Kneschke (crb). **Getty Images / iStock:** E+ / vgajic (cl). **215 123RF.com:** dmstudio (tr); fotana (bl). **216 Alamy Stock Photo:** NASA Photo (bl). **216-217 Alamy Stock Photo:** Sciepro / Science Photo Library. **217 123RF.com:** weenvector (ca). **Alamy Stock Photo:** 2020 Images (b); ZUMA Press, Inc. (tl). **Dreamstime.com:** Evgenii Naumov (crb); John Takai (cra); Topgeek (br). **218 Dreamstime.com:** Bulychevaart (bl). **220 123RF.com:** Roman Samborskyi (br). **Dreamstime.com:** Andrii Bezvershenko (fbl). **Getty Images:** Photodisc / Zing Images (bl). **222 Dreamstime.com:** Sebastian Kaulitzki (r). **224 Dreamstime.com:** Valentyn75 (br)

Cover images: *Front:* **123RF.com:** Volodimir Kalina tc; **Dreamstime.com:** Valentyn75 tl; *Back:* **123RF.com:** dmstudio tc; **Dreamstime.com:** Sjgh tl

All other images © Dorling Kindersley

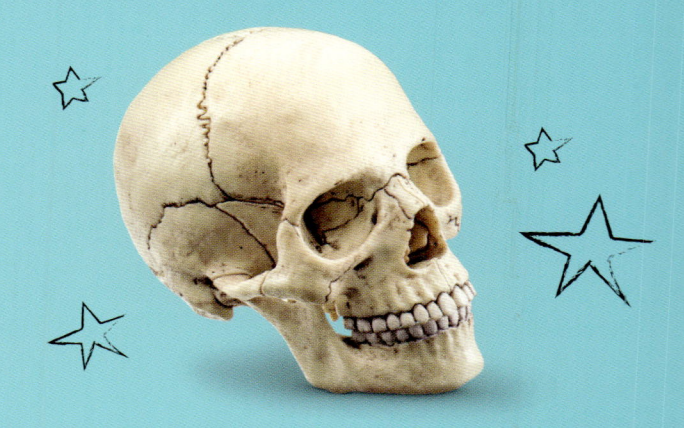